See-Me-Learn
TOYS

See-Me-Learn
TOYS

BY JENNIFER GEIGER

SEDGEWOOD® PRESS
New York, N.Y.

ACKNOWLEDGMENTS

Thanks to Betty Rice for her outstanding professional
expertise, warmth, and enthusiasm.
And to Lane Berkwit for the photographs in the book,
and for her good humor.
And thank you, Tony Hull, for being extremely patient and
helpful in selecting fabrics.
Editorial Director: Dina von Zweck

Laura Ashley fabrics are used as background for
the photos on pages 28, 76, 109, 124, 129, 153.

For Sedgewood® Press
Director: Elizabeth P. Rice
Project Editor: Barbara S. Machtiger
Production Manager: Bill Rose
Design: Antler & Baldwin Design Group

*The authors and publishers disclaim liability for injuries caused
by toys made according to instructions printed herein. Any toys should be
used only under adult supervision.*

Distributed by Meredith Corporation
ISBN: 0-696-02311-3

Library of Congress Catalog Card Number: 88-061379

Printed in the United States of America

10 9 8 7 6 5 4 3 2 1

To my son, Ian,
who inspired this book.

Contents

Introduction

See-Me-Learn Toys is a treasury of delightful soft toys to make for young children. They're colorful and appealing—and they're toys that will help develop your child's natural creativity and build important learning skills. They've been designed to expand imagination, intelligence, and self-confidence.

Whether your child is an infant or a toddler, he'll enjoy the day-to-day activities these toys provide. Twirl the Flying Acrobats Mobile around so your baby can respond to the blue and pink figures. Show your toddler how the five "peas" go in and out of the pod, in Five Peas in a Pod—and teach him the numbers 1 to 5. Teach your child colors with the Teach-Me-Colors Book. My son, Ian, who is two, loves Mr. Shapey. I've taught him the names of the shapes, and now he can Velcro the shapes on and off all by himself.

Dr. David Elking, president of the National Association for the Education of Young Children, says, "Young children learn best from their own experience. Young children learn from activity, from exploring real objects, talking to people, and solving real problems such as how to balance a stack of blocks or how to negotiate a zipper."

In childhood, it's the small moments of tender interaction between parent and child that count. With more than 40 projects in the book, there are many ways you can open the doors to the fun of learning for your child.

The projects are all fairly simple to make, and a few of them can be made from scraps. I've used colors and fabrics that I like—and that children respond to—but any bright fabric can be used.

You will find general sewing instructions and other helpful information in the General Directions section. Each project has an introduction that tells you about the teaching aspect of the toy and gives some practical guidance as well.

Any of the toys in this book would make a wonderful gift—so grandmothers, aunts, and friends, get out your sewing machines too. In this age of mass production, it's always a pleasure to receive a gift that's been handmade with love.

A few of these toys lend themselves to "multiples" and would make fine bazaar best-sellers.

I hope you enjoy making these very special toys as much as I enjoyed creating them. See-Me-Learn Toys was fun to put together as a book—and now I leave the fun of making them to you.

—J. G.

PRELIMINARIES

Basic Tools and Equipment

Here is a list of the items you will need to make the toys in this book.

Assorted needles: Sharps for hand sewing, embroidery needles for embroidery.

Beeswax: for coating hand-sewing thread to reduce knotting or tangling.

Blunt-end knitting needle: for turning stitched objects right side out and for stuffing small, hard-to-reach areas.

Circle template: for drawing and cutting out eyes and small circles.

Compass: for drawing circles.

Craft glue: for gluing on facial features.

Dressmaker's pins: for holding fabric in place while sewing.

Dressmaker's shears: bent handle shears with 7″ or 8″ blades for cutting fabric.

Dressmaker's carbon paper: for marking fabric and transferring designs.

Embroidery floss, six-strand: for stitching facial features. Use three strands.

Embroidery hoop, small: for holding fabric while embroidering faces.

Embroidery scissors: small scissors with 3″ or 4″ blades for more accurate trimming of threads and for cutting small pieces of fabric.

Felt-tip pens: for enlarging and marking patterns.

Graph or quadrille paper: for enlarging patterns.

Paper scissors: for cutting paper patterns.

Pencils, tailor's chalk, slivers of worn soap, pastel pencils: for marking fabric.

Polyester stuffing: for stuffing toys. Use one that is soft, fluffy, and of even consistency.

Ruler, 12″, see-through plastic with clearly marked numbers: for enlarging patterns and measuring fabric.

Safety pins: for drawing elastic through casing and turning fabric tubes.

Seam ripper: for ripping out unwanted stitches.

Sewing machine: for sewing toys in this book.

Sewing thread: dual duty, all-purpose thread for hand and machine sewing.

Steam iron and ironing board: for pressing fabric. Always press fabric before starting a project.

Tape measure: for measuring three-dimensional objects and fabric.

Thimble: for hand sewing to protect middle finger of hand guiding the needle.

Tracing paper: for transferring and enlarging patterns.

General Directions

Before making any of the projects in this book, read the General Directions to familiarize yourself with the basic techniques used. Some individual project directions refer to the General Directions for more detailed instruction.

How to Enlarge Patterns

To enlarge the patterns in this book you will need a grid of 1″ squares. To make a master grid that can be used repeatedly, simply use a pencil and a ruler to mark a grid of 1″ squares on a large sheet of paper (approximately 14″ × 18″). Small sheets of paper can be taped together to form one large sheet. You can also purchase sheets of blue graph or quadrille paper at an art supply store. And some sewing supply stores sell a special 1″ grid paper made for enlarging patterns.

To enlarge a pattern, tape a piece of tracing paper that is big enough to fit the final pattern onto the master grid. Using dots to mark where the pattern lines intersect, copy the reduced pattern, square by square, onto the enlarged grid. Connect the dots on the enlarged grid to get the final pattern drawing. Draw any other pattern markings onto the pattern. Cut out the pattern.

If you want to enlarge an individual pattern without making a master grid, just draw a grid directly onto whatever paper you plan to use. Then draw this pattern directly onto the grid. To make a pattern larger or smaller, just increase or reduce the size of the squares on the grid. *Note:* Each grid square pictured in this book equals ½″, or half the size of the actual pattern.

How to Choose Fabrics

Specific fabrics are listed for each toy project. Other fabrics may be substituted for these, but to ensure the best results the same types of fabrics should be used. When in doubt, use your own judgment or consult a salesperson.

With the exception of those that teach specific colors, different prints or colors may be substituted for most projects. If you change the suggested fabric color, be sure to coordinate all other fabrics and notions as well.

How to Press Fabrics

Press all fabrics before starting a project. Press fake fur and napped fabric on the wrong side. Test-iron on a scrap of fabric to prevent scorching or crushing fabric. Press all seams, hems, folds, and other fabric parts when indicated in the instructions. This saves time in the long run because it makes sewing easier and more accurate. It also gives the finished project a more professional look.

How to Transfer Patterns and Pattern Markings onto Fabric

Before you begin to cut out the patterns, press the fabric and check the grain line. Lay the fabric out on a large, flat surface. If instructions indicate that the fabric should be folded double, fold it with the selvage edges together. Place pattern pieces on the fabric as close together as possible. Line up the straight grain of the fabric with the top and bottom of each pattern piece. Place patterns marked "place on fold" on the fold of the fabric. Pin patterns into place on the fabric. With a pencil, tailor's chalk or sliver of soap, draw an outline of each pattern piece onto the fabric.

Before transferring pattern markings onto the fabric, decide which side is to be marked. Most dots and darts are marked on the wrong side, while facial features, pocket placement, and other pattern markings are marked on the right side of the fabric. Place dressmaker's carbon paper between the pattern and the fabric. Trace markings directly onto the fabric.

Some pattern markings can be temporarily marked with a pin placed through the pattern and the fabric. Carefully lift the pattern, then replace the pin by a pencil marking. Many fabrics are thin enough to allow you to trace the pattern markings through the material. A sunny window or light box may also be used. Tape the pattern to the glass, then tape the fabric over it. Trace over the pattern markings.

Fabrics like fake fur, corduroy, and velour have a nap. When the nap runs down, the fabric feels smooth. When cutting patterns, be sure the nap runs in the same direction.

Note: When cutting fake fur, have a vacuum cleaner handy to clean up flying fur.

How to Stitch the Toys in This Book

MACHINE STITCHING

Most of the projects in this book were sewn with a sewing machine using a straight or zigzag stitch. A small amount of hand stitching and embroidery was also used. When straight stitching, set the sewing machine at twelve stitches per inch. To prevent skipped stitches, use the proper size needle for each fabric.

Machine Zigzag Stitching. This stitch is used to join fabric pieces together, for embroidery, to machine appliqué, or to finish an edge. For best results, follow the directions that come with your sewing machine.

Machine Topstitching. This decorative stitch is used to join two pieces of fabric together. On the right side of the fabric, make a row of stitches the desired distance from the fabric edge or seam. Stitch through the entire fabric.

HAND STITCHING

Slipstitch. This almost invisible stitch is used to join two folded edges of a fabric, to hem and to hold ears, pockets, and other features in place. Slip the needle through the folded edge of the fabric. Make a small stitch through the under fabric, then slip the needle back through the folded edge. When stitching two folded edges, slip the needle back and forth through the fabric folds. Space stitches evenly at ⅛″ to ¼″.

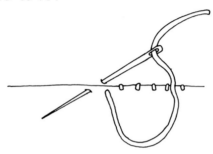

Running Stitch. This stitch is used for basting, gathering, mending, quilting, or hand sewing seams that are not subjected to much strain.

Work the needle in and out of the fabric until there are several tiny, even stitches on it. Pull the needle and thread through the fabric and start the next series of stitches.

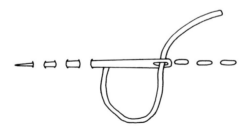

EMBROIDERY STITCHES

Embroidery is used to stitch many of the facial features on projects in this book. Use three strands of the six-strand embroidery floss when stitching to allow for easier insertion of thread into the fabric and to achieve more accurate results.

To "lose an end" when embroidering faces on stuffed projects, embroider the features as usual, knotting the end by overstitching. Place the needle back into the fabric, through the stuffing, and out about 1″ away. Pull the thread taut and clip it close to the fabric.

Backstitch. This stitch is used for sewing strong seams and embroidery outlines.

Begin at the right end of the line to be covered or seam to be sewn. Bring the needle through the fabric to the right side. Insert the needle back into the fabric ⅛″ behind the starting point. Bring the needle back through the right side of the fabric ⅛″ in front of the starting point. Continue inserting the needle back to the last stitch and bringing it out one stitch ahead.

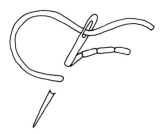

Satin Stitch. This stitch is used to cover such areas as noses and mouths with stitches. It is made by filling in an area with closely spaced parallel stitches. Before starting, draw an outline around the area to be covered, then work within these guidelines.

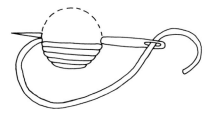

French Knot. This stitch is used to make freckles and small dots for eyes and noses.

Pull the thread through to the right side of the fabric, and with your free hand, wrap the thread tightly around the needle four or five times depending on the desired size of the knot. Insert the needle back into the fabric close to the point where the thread emerged. Pull the needle through the wrapped thread to the wrong side of the fabric.

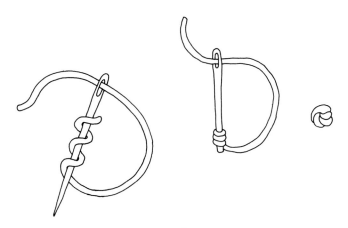

How to Clip, Notch, and Trim Seam Allowance

To prevent curved stitched seams from puckering or pulling, clip inwardly curved seams almost to the seam allowance. For outwardly curved seams, notch by cutting out small wedges of fabric to eliminate bulkiness.

Before turning stitched pieces right side out, trim the seam allowance diagonally at the corners to create less bulk and achieve a sharper corner.

How to Stuff Projects

The projects in this book are stuffed with polyester stuffing.

Stuff small, hard-to-reach areas first, using a knitting needle or chopstick to prod bits of stuffing into place. Stuff larger areas using handfuls of stuffing and working your way out to the fabric opening. To avoid lumps and bumps, stuff projects firmly and evenly.

How to Bind Edges

Lining up the raw edges, place fabric strip or bias tape right sides together with the fabric. If the ends of the binding meet, fold one end under ¼″ and overlap it with the opposite end. Stitch the fabric to the binding with a ¼″ seam or as specified. Turn the binding over the seam allowance. Fold the edge of the binding strip under so it is even with the stitching line. Slipstitch the folded edge of the binding to the fabric.

How to Attach Small Objects

Use extreme care when attaching small objects such as bells, buttons, snaps, and pompons. These must be securely stitched, using double thread. Check periodically to make sure stitching is still secure and reattach object if necessary.

Some facial features are glued into place. Instead of gluing, these can often be stitched into place. Whether glued or stitched, however, facial features should be checked periodically and reattached if necessary.

If neither gluing nor stitching is desired, facial features can be embroidered directly onto the project. First draw an outline of the shape, then fill it in with a satin stitch.

PROJECTS

Flying Acrobats Mobile

This "look and listen" toy gives the newborn something cheerful to focus on. The bells encourage baby to respond to sound and, as he looks at what he hears, he will learn to coordinate sight and sound. The mobile will encourage a young baby's curiosity, as he lifts his head and uses his eyes to follow the flying acrobats. This is an excellent first toy, and it can be made before baby's birth to decorate the nursery. It's a time-consuming project but is well worth the effort. And it can be handed down from one child to the next.

MATERIALS

9″ × 30″ piece light blue cotton fabric
¼ yard pink cotton fabric
1¾ yards 1″-wide embroidered trim
1½ yards yellow rickrack, medium width
1 yard 1¾″-wide eyelet lace, ungathered
2 yards ⅝″-wide yellow satin ribbon
1½ yards each of ⅛″-wide yellow and pink satin
 ribbon
7″ hoop (inside ring of embroidery hoop,
 framing hoop, or any craft hoop)
Polyester stuffing
Four round bells
Thread to match fabrics

See How to Enlarge Patterns in General Directions, page 12.

Enlarge and cut patterns from paper. Cut four acrobats each from pink and blue fabrics. Cut eight hearts from pink fabric. Cut rickrack into two 8″ pieces, two 11″ pieces, and four 4″ pieces.

Pin 11″ piece of rickrack to seam allowance on foot of two blue acrobats. Pin 8″ piece of rickrack to seam allowance on hand of two pink acrobats. See pattern. With right sides together and rickrack between layers, machine-stitch pairs of pink and pairs of blue acrobats with ¼″ seam allowance. Leave 2″ opening on one side for turning. Clip curves and turn right side out. Stuff and slipstitch opening closed.

19

Pin 4″ piece of rickrack to seam allowance of four hearts. With right sides together, machine-stitch pairs of hearts with ¼″ seam allowance. Leave 2″ opening on one side for turning. Clip curves and turn right side out. Stuff and slipstitch opening closed.

Cut eyelet lace into two equal lengths and gather evenly along each top raw edge. Cut two 6″ pieces of embroidered trim. Place ¼″ raw edge of lace under trim and machine-topstitch. Stitch ends of each piece together to form skirt. Slip skirt over legs of each pink acrobat and position at waist. Tack into place.

Cut two 12″ pieces each from ⅛″-wide yellow and pink ribbon. Fold each piece in half and stitch 2¾″ from fold to form a loop. Slip both a yellow and a pink loop around waist of each blue acrobat.

Cut remaining pink and yellow ⅛″-wide ribbons in half. Tie a yellow bow around each pink neck and a pink bow around each blue neck.

Cut two 22½″ pieces of 1″-wide trim. With ¼″

seam allowance, stitch ends together to form two circles. Press seams open.

Evenly spaced at 5½″ intervals, pin free end of each acrobat's rickrack piece to inside of one trim circle. Center and pin free end of each heart's rickrack between acrobats. Place remaining trim circle inside pinned trim circle and topstitch the two together along bottom edge, catching rickrack as you sew.

Cut yellow ⅝″-wide ribbon into three 24″ pieces. Evenly spaced at 6¾″ intervals, pin one end of each ribbon inside the top trim opening. Insert pin through one layer only. Place the 7″ hoop inside the opening and slipstitch trim closed, catching ribbon ends as you sew.

Stitch all three pieces of ⅝″-wide yellow ribbon together 11″ above the hoop. Fold remainder of one ribbon in half, attach end at 3-ribbon joining to form hanging loop. Tie a bow with the remaining two ends of yellow ribbon.

Stitch a bell to a hand or a foot of each acrobat.

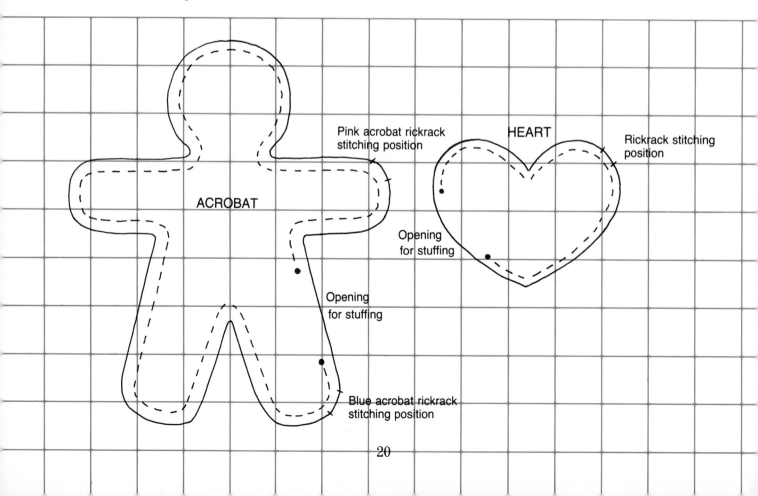

Baby Bunnies Crib Toy

*These happy little bunnies are a classic "look
and touch" toy. They can be hung on a crib or playpen
within easy reach of baby. The toy encourages baby
to explore the world around her, to reach out and
touch what she sees. It improves hand-eye coordination
and develops motor skills.
I've made this in a heart-motif fabric, but any fabric
with a small print would be just as appealing.*

MATERIALS

Cotton fabrics:
6″ × 6½″ piece green
6″ × 10″ piece orange
¼ yard 45″-wide blue print

1 yard each six-strand pink and black
    embroidery floss
Three 1½″ pompons
Polyester stuffing
3 yards ⅞″-wide satin ribbon
Thread to match fabrics

See How to Enlarge Patterns in General
Directions, page 12.
Enlarge pattern pieces; cut from paper.

Fold green and orange fabrics in half. From
green fabric, cut two pairs of carrot tops. From
orange fabric, cut two pairs of carrots.

With right sides together, stitch carrot tops
with ⅛″ seam, leaving bottom open. Clip seam
allowance, turn right side out, and stuff lightly.
Following pattern, topstitch stems onto carrot-
tops (broken lines).

With right sides together stitch carrots with
⅛″ seam, leaving top open. Turn right side out
and stuff. Turn raw edges of carrot under ⅛″
Pin, then slipstitch carrot top inside carrot
opening.

With blue print fabric folded double, cut three
pairs of bunnies. Following pattern, lightly draw
a face in pencil on one bunny from each set. Use
a different facial expression for each bunny.

21

See Embroidery Stitches in General Directions, page 14.

Using a satin stitch, fill in eyes with black embroidery floss and noses with pink. Backstitch with pink floss over mouth drawing.

With right sides together, stitch pairs of bunnies with ¼" seams. Leave 2" opening along one side for stuffing. Clip curves in seam allowance, turn right side out, and stuff. Slipstitch opening closed.

Spread pompon fibers apart so center staple is visible. Using double thread securely stitch a pompon to center bottom of each bunny, stitching through the center of pompon staple.

Using small, closely placed stitches, slipstitch carrots to bunny paws. Alternate bunnies and carrots.

Divide ribbon into two equal pieces. Fold each piece in half and crease with thumbnail. Open ribbon and backstitch securely along the fold to the paws of two outside bunnies. Stitch back and forth a few times.

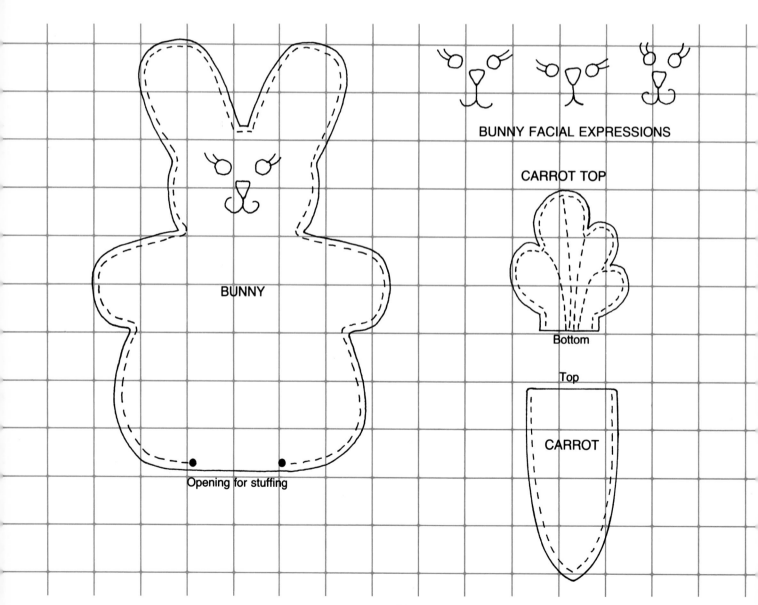

BUNNY FACIAL EXPRESSIONS

CARROT TOP

Bottom

Top

CARROT

BUNNY

Opening for stuffing

Golden Sun Rattle

All babies love to shake rattles. Reaching and grasping are new skills at about six months. When baby learns to shake the rattle and make noise, he's learning to influence the environment by controlling objects around him.
The bright colors and smiling face stimulate sight and touch. The toy strengthens baby's grip and develops hand manipulation. When baby focuses on the rattle's face, he is also developing an ability to concentrate.

MATERIALS

Felt fabrics:
3½″ × 3½″ piece white
1″ × 2″ pieces light pink, dark pink, light blue, and black
8″ × 16″ piece yellow-and-white polka dot cotton fabric
3½″ × 3½″ piece fusible interfacing
Six 1″-diameter pompons
1½ yards six-strand black embroidery floss
Few handfuls polyester stuffing
Three bells
Craft glue
White thread and thread to match cotton fabric

See How To Enlarge Patterns in General Directions, page 12.

Enlarge A and B pattern pieces, drawing face on A. Cut from paper.

Trace facial features onto another piece of paper and use drawing as pattern. From felt, cut out one dark-pink mouth and two light-pink cheeks, light-blue irises, and black pupils.

Cut out one A piece from both white felt and fusible interfacing. Using A pattern as a guide, draw eyebrows, eye outline, nose, and chin on felt. Glue mouth and eyes into place. When glue is dry, backstitch over drawn lines with black embroidery floss. See Backstitch instructions in General Directions, page 14. With a hot iron, ad-

24

here fusible interfacing to back of A.

Cut two B pieces from cotton fabric. Center A on one of the B pieces. Pin and slipstitch into place.

With right sides together machine-stitch around edge of B pieces, using ¼″ seam allowance and leaving 2″ opening for turning. Clip seam allowances and trim excess fabric at points. Turn right side out and fill with polyester stuffing. Embed bells into stuffing in center of B to make rattle. Slipstitch opening closed.

Push the pompon fibers apart to see center staple. Sew the pompon securely to end of each ray by stitching through and over the staple.

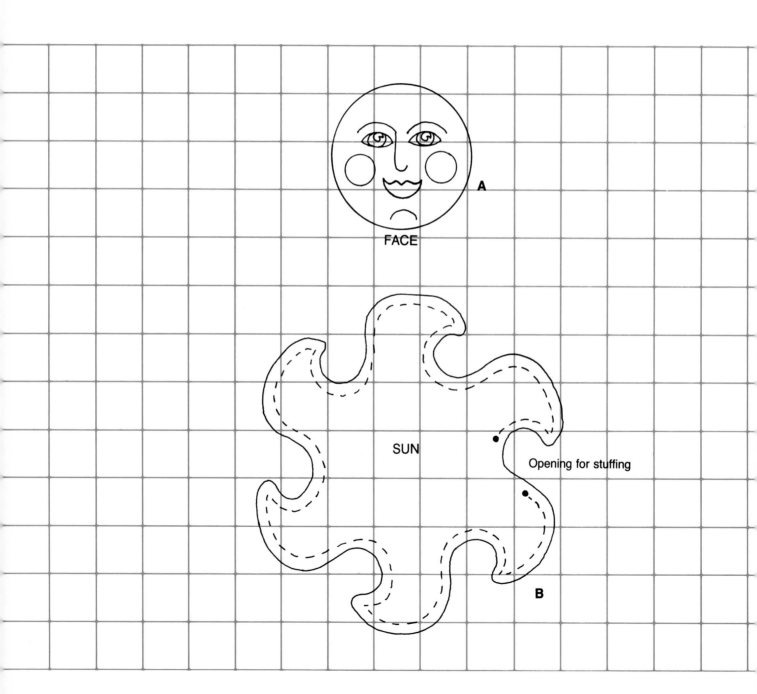

FACE

A

SUN

Opening for stuffing

B

Ice-Cream-Cone Baby

Each of these adorable pastel babies in soft flannel nightshirts has a rattle in its ice-cream cone and a bell in its hat. The small cone can be fastened and unfastened with Velcro to help develop baby's motor control and coordination. Ice-Cream-Cone Babies stimulate sight, sound, and touch. They're not only soft and cuddly but make imaginative companions as baby grows.

MATERIALS

Cotton fabrics:
8½" × 18" piece rust
5" × 10" piece pastel
3½" × 6" piece contrasting pastel
10" × 14" piece flannel print

21" piece gathered eyelet lace, 1" wide
12" satin ribbon, ⅝" wide
Few handfuls polyester stuffing
Six-strand embroidery floss (red, blue, and
    black)
⅝" Velcro circle
Two round bells
Thread to match fabrics

See How to Enlarge Patterns in General Directions, page 12.

Enlarge pattern pieces and cut from paper. Letter each pattern. Draw neck stitching line on patterns A and B. Draw face on B.

Cut two A pieces from rust fabric and two B pieces from pastel fabric. All seams are ¼". With right sides together, place a B piece on each A piece, lining up neck stitching lines, and machine-stitch. Press seams open. Trace face onto right side of one B piece.

See Embroidery Stitches in General Directions, page 14.

With red embroidery floss, backstitch mouth and nose. With black embroidery floss, backstitch

eye outline. With blue embroidery floss, fill in irises with satin stitch. To make pupils, stitch four small horizontal stitches on irises with black embroidery floss.

With right sides together pin, then machine-stitch Ice-Cream-Cone Baby. Leave 3″ opening along one side of body. Clip seam allowances and turn right side out. Fill with polyester stuffing and slipstitch opening closed.

From flannel fabric, cut two C and D pieces. Press neckline, sleeve, and bottom edge of each C piece under ¼″. Press bottom edge of each D piece under ¼″.

Machine-hem neckline and sleeves on each C piece. Then place right sides together and machine-stitch shoulder and side seams. Turn right side out and stitch lace to turned bottom edge.

Tie a bow with satin ribbon and stitch to center front of shirt ¼″ below neckline.

With right sides together machine-stitch D pieces, leaving bottom edge open. Turn right side out and stitch lace to turned bottom edge. Place bell inside tip of hat, then fill loosely with walnut-size piece of polyester stuffing. Bell should be loose enough to ring.

Position hat on Baby's head and slipstitch into place.

Cut two cones from rust fabric and two ice creams from constrasting pastel fabric. With right sides together and raw edges lined up, stitch an ice cream to top of each cone. With right sides together stitch ice-cream cone, leaving a 1″ opening along one side of cone. Turn right side out and fill with polyester stuffing, embedding a bell inside cone. Slipstitch opening closed. Slipstitch one side of Velcro circle to baby's hand. Center and slipstitch remaining Velcro side to ice-cream cone.

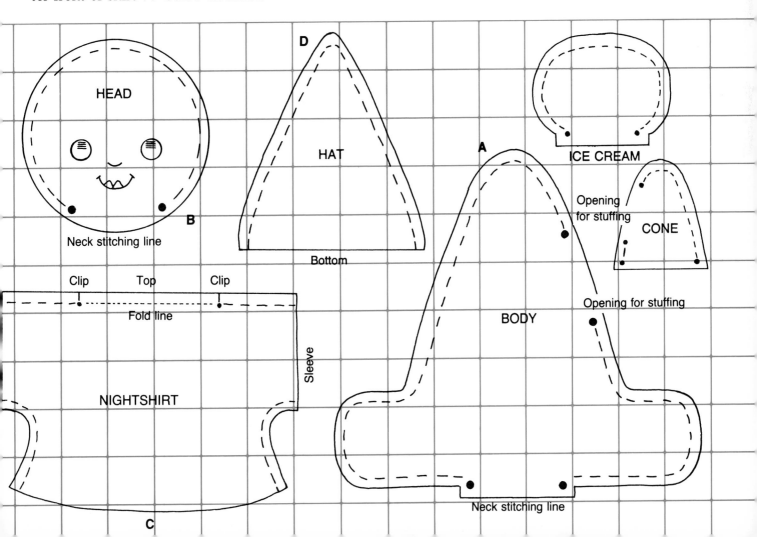

Nesting Hen and Chicks

*This "hide and find" design is a favorite childhood toy.
It's soft and fluffy, and the two little chicks hide
almost inside the mother's wings. This toy introduces
baby to the concept of object permanence. She learns
that objects do not cease to exist simply because
they are out of sight.*
*The chicks hide and reappear. Peekaboo. And baby can
place the chicks where they belong all by herself.
Object placement helps the child develop a strong
sense of self.*

MATERIALS

¼ yard 58"-wide fake fur
8" × 12" piece orange cotton fabric
8" × 10" piece yellow cotton fabric
Small scrap black felt
½ yard picot-edge satin ribbon, ½" wide
¾ yard picot-edge satin ribbon, ¼" wide
Polyester stuffing
Thread to match fabrics
Craft glue

See How To Enlarge Patterns in General
Directions, page 12.

Enlarge pattern pieces and cut from paper.
Letter each pattern. Mark notches and top wing
placement dots on the A pieces.

With nap running down cut two A pieces (cut
one, reverse pattern, then cut one more), one B
piece, and four C pieces (cut two, reverse pattern, then cut two more) from fake fur. Mark dots
in seam allowances and mark top wing placement
dots on both A pieces with pins.

From orange fabric cut two D, E, and F pieces,
and four G pieces. All seams are ¼". With right
sides together, machine-stitch D, E, F, and G
pieces, leaving straight sides open. Clip seam allowances, turn right side out, and press. Fill each
piece with polyester stuffing.

To make Nesting Hen, line up raw edges, and baste D, E, F, and one G to seam allowance of one A piece. Baste second G piece to seam allowance of remaining A piece.

With right sides together machine-stitch C pieces, leaving 2½" opening along bottom. Turn right side out and slipstitch opening closed. Pin, then slipstitch a C piece into place on each A piece, lining up top of each wing with wing placement dots on A. Top edge of wings will be slightly larger than markings on A. Sides of each wing must be pushed in to create a gap that will allow chicks to be inserted.

With right sides together and lining up dots, pin B in place around bottom of one A piece and machine-stitch, easing B around the curves. Pin, then machine-stitch the remaining A piece to unstitched side of A and B pieces. Leave 4" opening along side. Turn right side out and fill with polyester stuffing. Slipstitch opening closed.

To make chicks from yellow fabric, cut four H pieces. Mark dots. Cut four I pieces from orange fabric. With right sides together, line up raw edges, stitch an I piece to each H piece. Press I pieces (beaks) away from H pieces (bodies). With right sides together stitch H pieces, leaving 2½" opening along side. Turn right side out and fill with polyester stuffing. Slipstitch opening closed.

From black felt, cut round eyes for hen and chicks. Glue into place.

Wrap ½"-wide ribbon around hen's neck, crossing one side over other under wattle, and tack into place with a few small stitches.

Cut ¼"-wide ribbon in half and tie a bow around each chick's neck. Secure bows by sewing a few stitches through center knot.

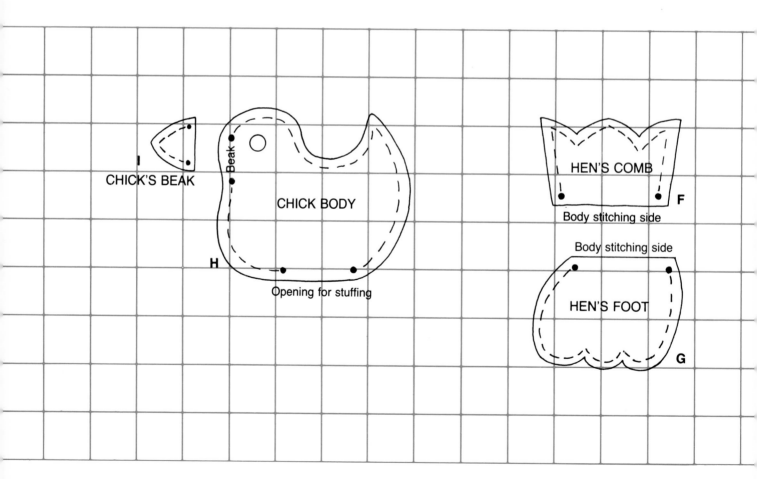

CHICK'S BEAK · I

Beak

CHICK BODY

H

Opening for stuffing

HEN'S COMB

F

Body stitching side

Body stitching side

HEN'S FOOT

G

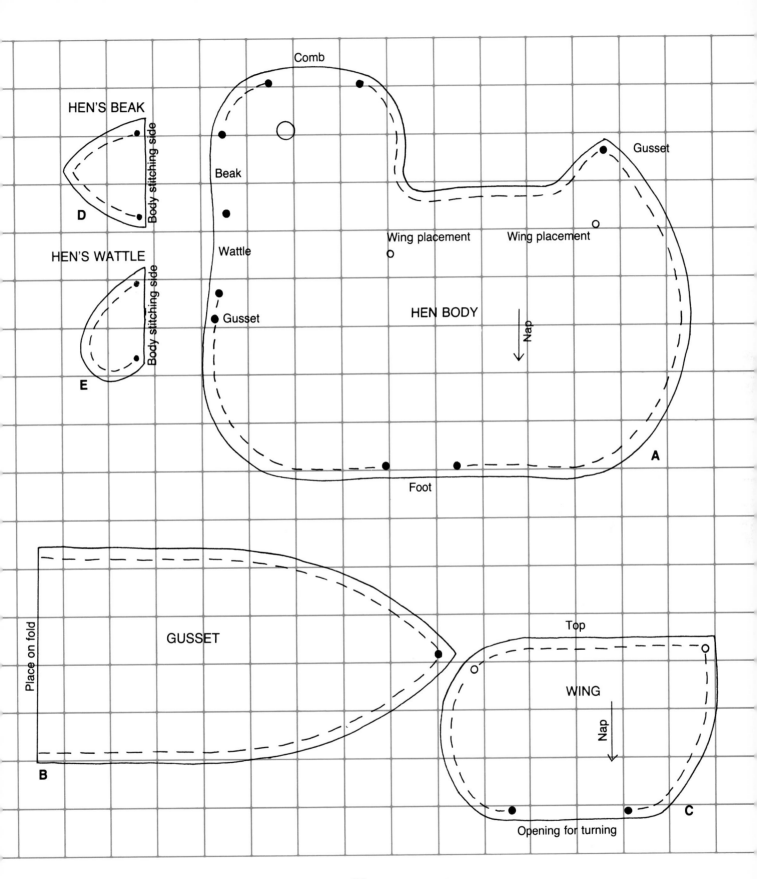

HEN'S BEAK

D

HEN'S WATTLE

E

Body stitching side

Comb

Beak

Wattle

Gusset

Wing placement

Wing placement

Gusset

HEN BODY

Nap

Foot

A

GUSSET

Place on fold

B

Top

WING

Nap

Opening for turning

C

Teeter Tower

Blocks are one of the most basic toys for toddlers. This set develops size and shape relationships and is a good precounting activity. The soft blocks keep active hands busy and have the advantage of not hurting baby when they fall down. As your child learns to recognize the differences in the size of the blocks, she will learn how to stack them so they don't topple over. It's a problem-solving toy that your child can play with all by herself.
The Teeter Tower is an ideal bazaar item because it is easy to make from fabric scraps and can be made in multiples by relatively inexperienced seamstresses. Any bright cotton prints can be used.

MATERIALS

Cotton fabrics:
6″ block—2½″ × 20″ strip print
       6½″ × 12½″ piece print
5″ block—2½″ × 17″ strip print
       5½″ × 10½″ piece print
4″ block—2½″ × 13″ strip print
       4½″ × 8½″ piece print
3″ block—2½″ × 10″ strip print
       3½″ × 6½″ piece print
Polyester stuffing
Thread to match fabrics

See How to Enlarge Patterns in General Directions, page 12.

For each block, enlarge circle pattern and cut from paper. Cut two circles from fabric.

Press 2½″-side of fabric strip under ¼″. With right sides together and using ¼″ seam allowance, stitch fabric strip around outside edge of one circle piece. Fold back raw edge of strip end so folded ends meet. See Diagram A.

Stitch remaining circle piece to unstitched side of strip. Turn block right side out through opening on strip. Stuff. Slipstitch opening closed.

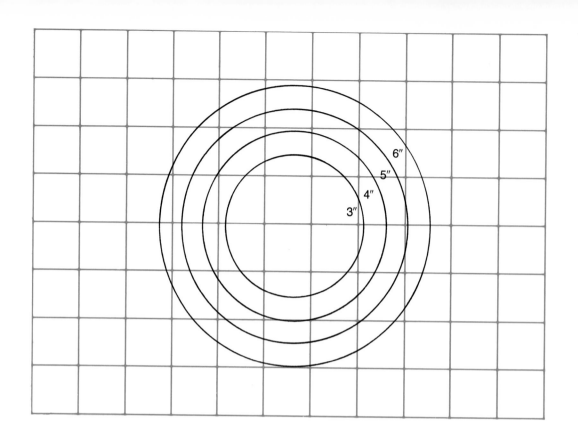

6"
5"
4"
3"

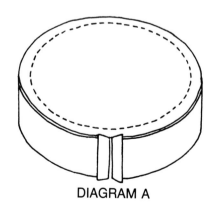

DIAGRAM A

Banana Babe

*The corduroy peel unzips to reveal Banana Babe,
a lovable creature that could easily become your
child's favorite toy. This is "seek and find" at
its most imaginative. It not only teaches the concept
of object permanence (Banana Babe still exists
when zippered inside the peel) but improves
coordination as your child learns how to open and
close the zipper and take Banana Babe in
and out of the peel.
Banana Babe is Mr. Personality Plus. With his winning
smile, he radiates happiness. It won't be hard for
a child to identify with that enduring quality.
This is a moderately easy project. If you prefer, you
can make the peel out of thin sweatshirt fleece instead
of the corduroy shown.*

MATERIALS

¼ yard 45″-wide yellow corduroy
¼ yard 45″-wide yellow cotton
¼ yard white robe velour
6″ × 8″ piece black felt
18″ jacket zipper
2 yards white yarn
Polyester stuffing
Yellow and black threads
Craft glue

See How to Enlarge Patterns in General
Directions, page 12.

Enlarge and cut pattern pieces from paper.
Fold yellow corduroy in half, with nap running
down, and pin banana peel pattern to fabric. Cut
two peel pieces. Cut two peel pieces from yellow
cotton, also folded double. Mark all dots.

Following pattern and using black thread and
closely spaced small zigzag stitch, stitch three
horizontal lines on each corduroy banana piece.

Using double thread, securely bar-tack both sides of zipper together ¼" from bottom end to prevent it from opening completely. See Diagram A.

With right sides together, place a corduroy peel piece on a cotton peel piece. With outside of zipper facing corduroy, sandwich zipper between the two pieces. Line up one long, straight edge of zipper with top straight edge of peel. Positioning zipper between dots, machine-stitch all three layers together with ¼" seam allowance. See Diagram B.

Turn stitched peel right side out to expose unsewn side of zipper. Stitch remaining peel pieces to this side of zipper, corresponding to first peel pieces. Topstitch along both sides of zipper. See Diagram C.

Unzip and turn peel inside out (corduroy sides together) and machine-stitch around perimeter using ¼" seam allowance. Turn peel right side out and press.

Cut one banana bottom from black felt. Slipstitch to bottom end of peel.

For Banana Babe, cut two body pieces and two arms from velour. Cut four hands from black felt. All seams are ¼". Stitch arm side seams. Turn right side out. Lining up raw edges, baste arms to right side of one body piece.

Cut twelve 6" pieces of yarn. Fold each piece in half. Lining up folded edges of yarn with raw edge of fabric, stitch yarn to seam allowance of head on right side of front body piece. See Diagram D.

With right sides together stitch body pieces, leaving 4" opening along one side for stuffing. Turn right side out and stuff. Slipstitch opening closed. Trim yarn evenly.

Following pattern diagram, cut out facial features from felt and glue into place.

With wrong sides together and using closely spaced zigzag stitch, topstitch pairs of hands together. Leave straight side open. Stuff lightly. Insert arm end into hand opening. Zigzag-stitch opening closed.

For bow tie, cut two ties from yellow cotton and one 1" × 1½" strip. With right sides together, stitch tie pieces with ⅛" seam, leaving a 1½" opening along one side for turning. Turn right side out, press, and slipstitch opening closed.

Press both long sides of strip in so edges meet at center. Press strip in half lengthwise. Wrap strip around center bow tie, gathering tie fabric, and slipstitch ends together. Stitch tie securely to Banana Babe's neck.

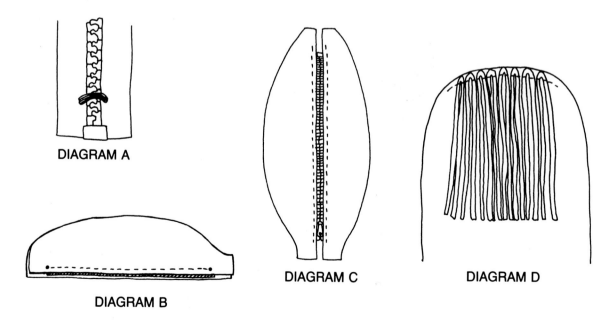

DIAGRAM A

DIAGRAM B

DIAGRAM C

DIAGRAM D

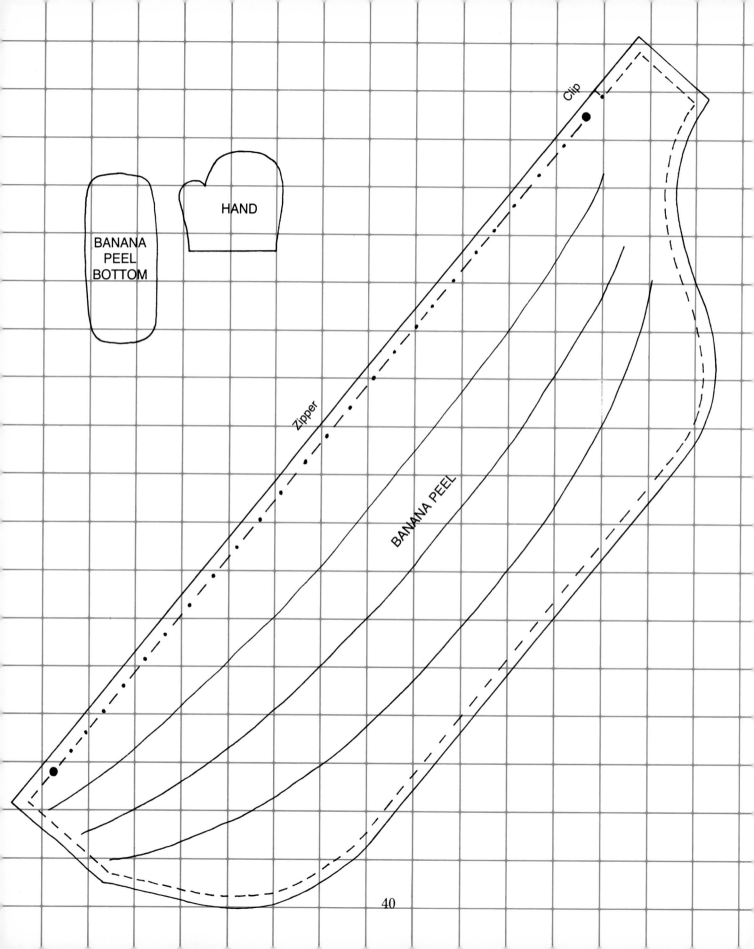

BANANA PEEL
BOTTOM

HAND

Clip

Zipper

BANANA PEEL

40

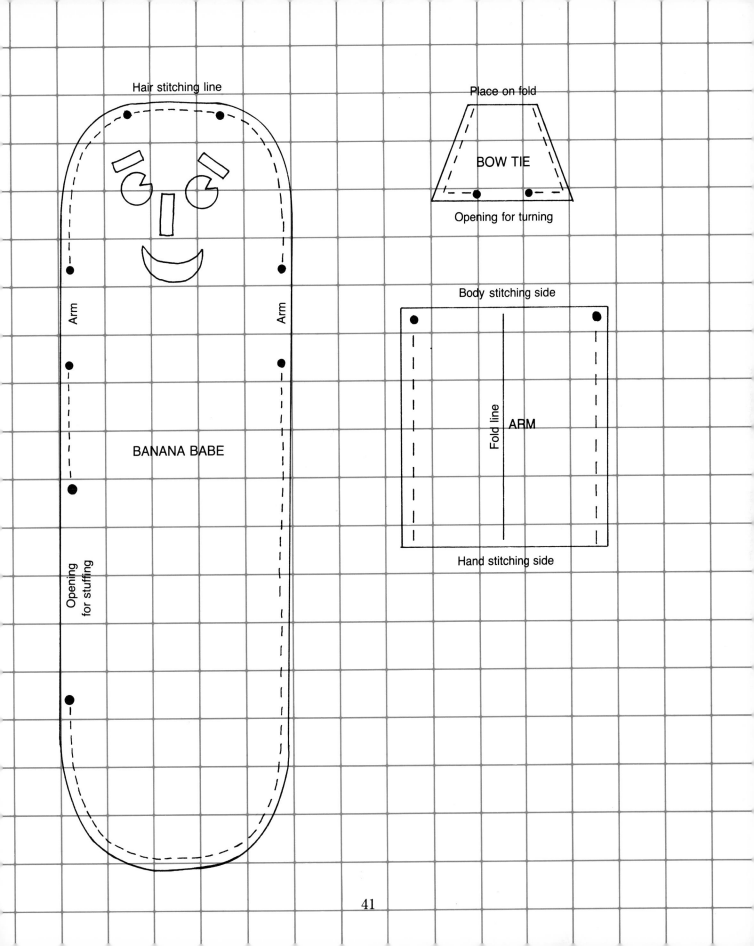

Hair stitching line

Place on fold

BOW TIE

Opening for turning

Arm

Arm

Body stitching side

Fold line   ARM

Hand stitching side

BANANA BABE

Opening
for stuffing

41

Who's Hiding? Peekaboo Book

Baby's first book stimulates curiosity. Instead of turning pages, your child can lift the flaps to see who's hiding. This simple book develops critical learning skills in a child's prereading years. For example, learning to recognize a bunny by seeing only one part of it not only develops understanding of part-whole relationships but also strengthens memory.

The Who's Hiding? Peekaboo Book encourages your child to make choices and direct his own actions. And even after he can easily remember who's hiding under the flaps, he'll still want to play with it because young children find the repetition and familiarity of the game extremely satisfying and rewarding.

MATERIALS

Cotton fabrics:
Two 7½″ × 26″ pieces orange
6″ × 15″ piece purple print
6″ × 15″ piece turquoise print
Felt fabrics:
5″ × 5″ piece each black and yellow
5″ × 3″ piece white
2″ × 4″ piece beige
6″ × 9″ piece blue

Small scrap each light pink and dark pink

7½″ × 26″ piece fusible interfacing
Two yellow feathers
Walnut-size piece of polyester stuffing
Two sets ⅝″ Velcro circles
10″ piece red yarn
Thread to match fabrics
Craft glue

See How to Enlarge Patterns in General Directions, page 12.

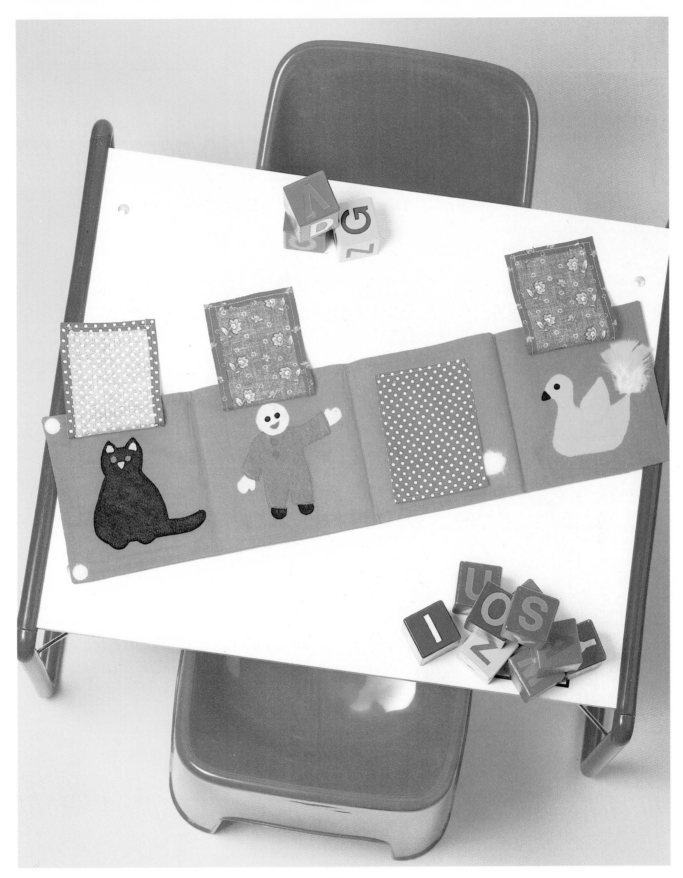

43

Enlarge pattern pieces and cut from paper. Divide one orange fabric piece into four equal panels by drawing vertical stitching lines 6½″ apart. On each panel mark 4″-long top flap stitching line 1″ below top and 1″ away from left side of panel. See Diagram A.

Cut out two flaps each from purple and turquoise fabrics. Cut four figures from felt: kitten from black, with light-pink nose and ears, and blue eyes; man's body from blue, with beige hands and head, black shoes and eyes, dark-pink buttons and mouth; bunny from white, with dark-pink nose, black eye, and light-pink ear; duckling from yellow, with yellow wing and black eye and beak.

For front cover, cut out man's head with eyes and mouth. From blue felt, cut out letters to spell "Who's Hiding?"

Press, then machine-stitch all flap edges under ¼″. Machine-stitch a flap into place on each panel, alternating colors.

Pin a felt figure under each flap so only tail (or hand) is visible when flap is down. Glue eyes, ears, hands, feet, and other body parts into place.

Glue feathers into place under duck's tail so ends are concealed under felt. Zigzag-stitch figures into place. Glue polyester stuffing to rabbit's tail.

With hot iron, adhere interfacing to remaining orange piece of fabric. With right sides together machine-stitch orange pieces with ¼″ seams, leaving 5″ opening along one end. Turn right side out and stitch opening closed. Press edges lightly.

Topstitch over vertical stitching lines and around perimeter of book ¼″ in from edges.

Slipstitch one side of a Velcro circle to top and bottom corner of left panel.

Starting with the right panel, fold the book into the closed position. Where Velcro circles fall on back panel, stitch opposite Velcro sides into place.

With book in closed position, arrange letters diagonally in two rows on outside panel. See Diagram B. Glue into place.

Cut red yarn into ten 1″ pieces. Glue yarn pieces to top underside of remaining man's head. Glue eyes and mouth into place. Glue entire head to bottom right-hand corner of outside panel.

DIAGRAM A

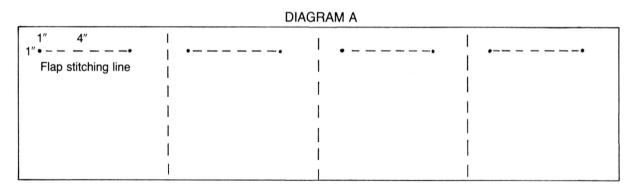

FRONT COVER

DIAGRAM B

Top

FLAP

BEAK

WING

KITTEN

DUCKLING

HEAD

HAND

MAN'S BODY

BUNNY

TAIL

FOOT

WHO'S HIDING?

Funny Face Fruit-in-a-Basket

Funny Face bean bags entertain and teach both babies and toddlers. Babies will love filling and emptying the basket. Toddlers will learn to name the fruits and enjoy tossing them into the basket, as they improve their hand-eye coordination.
The funny faces evoke happy and grumpy characters who will stimulate and enrich an active child's mind.

MATERIALS

Cotton fabrics:
9″ × 10″ piece red
5″ × 10″ piece orange
9″ × 13″ piece yellow
4″ × 4″ piece brown
8″ × 12″ piece green
⅜ yard 45″-wide blue print

⅜ yard 45″-wide fusible interfacing
5″ × 27″ piece and 9″ × 9″ piece extra-loft quilt
   batting
Handful polyester stuffing
1 pound small red or white dried beans
Six-strand black embroidery floss
Dressmaker's carbon paper
Thread to match fabrics

See How to Enlarge Patterns in General Directions, page 12.

Enlarge and cut patterns from paper. Draw faces and dots on fruit.

To construct fruit, place dressmaker's carbon paper right side down on fabric. Place fruit pattern on top and trace face and outside edge of fruit onto fabric. Repeat for each fruit pattern, making apple and strawberry red, orange orange, and lemon and banana yellow. Do not cut out fruit pieces.

See Embroidery Stitches in General Directions, page 14.

For each fruit piece, backstitch over eyebrows, eye outlines, noses, and mouths. Fill in pupils with satin stitch. Stitch French knots on strawberry to make freckles.

47

Cut out embroidered fruit pieces. Trace and cut another fruit piece for each fruit.

From brown fabric, cut four stems. From green fabric, cut three pairs of large leaves and three pairs of small leaves.

All seams are ⅛".

Fold stems in half. Stitch across one short side and long side. Using knitting needle or blunt pointed object, push fabric right side out.

Lining up raw edges, baste a stem to top dot on each embroidered fruit piece. With right sides together stitch fruit, leaving 2" opening for stuffing. Turn fruit right side out and press lightly.

Following Diagram A, make a paper funnel and insert small end into fruit opening. Pour beans into funnel, filling fruit with beans. Slipstitch openings closed.

Stitch leaves, leaving 1½" opening along one side. Turn right side out. Fill with polyester stuffing. Slipstitch opening closed.

Stitch large leaf to stem of orange, apple, and lemon. Stitch three small leaves to stem of strawberry. See Diagram B.

To construct basket, from blue print fabric cut out two 8" circles, two 4" × 26" strips, two 1½" × 26" strips, and one 1½" × 5" strip.

From interfacing, cut two 8" circles and two 4" × 26" strips. Fuse interfacing to blue fabric with hot iron.

On right side of one circle piece, mark parallel quilting lines 1" apart. On right side of one 4" × 26" strip, mark vertical parallel quilting lines 2" apart. See Diagram C.

Sandwich 9" × 9" piece batting between fabric circles. Baste layers together. Machine-quilt over drawn lines. Zigzag-stitch along outside edge of fabric. Trim excess batting.

Sandwich 5" × 27" piece of batting between 4" × 26" fabric strips. Baste layers together. Machine-quilt over drawn lines. Zigzag-stitch along outside edge of fabric. Trim excess batting.

See How to Bind Edges in General Directions, page 16.

Stitch short side of quilted strip with ¼" seam. Bind seam allowance with 1½" × 5" fabric strip.

Baste, then machine-stitch circle piece to one end of stitched strip with ¼" seam. Bind seam allowance along bottom edge and top raw edge of basket with 1½" × 26" strips.

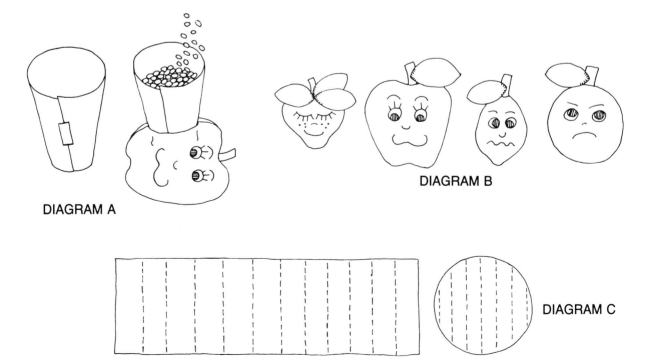

DIAGRAM A

DIAGRAM B

DIAGRAM C

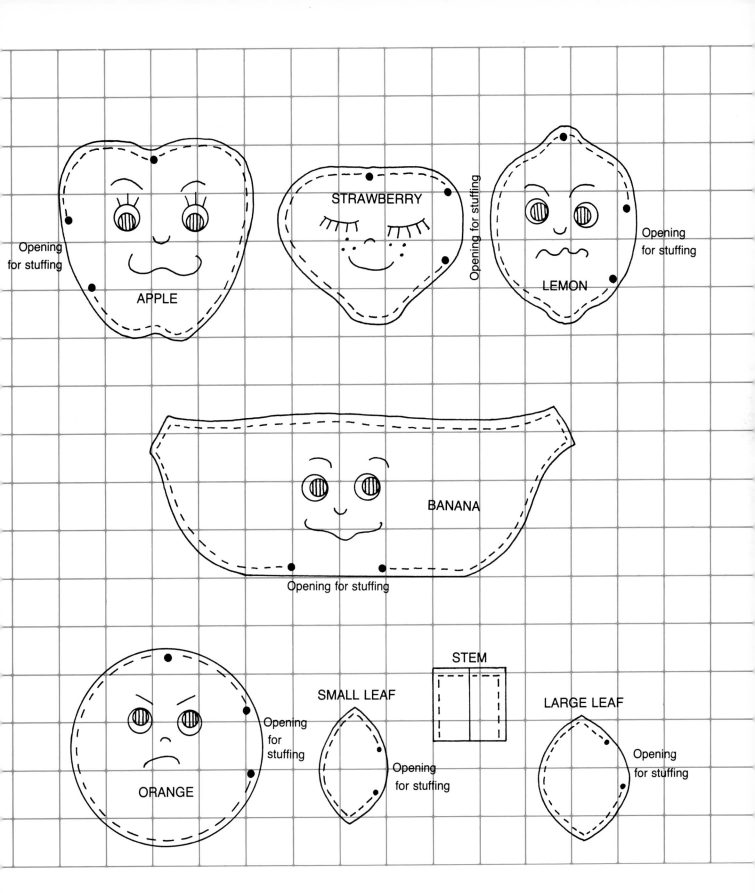

STRAWBERRY

Opening for stuffing

Opening for stuffing

LEMON

Opening for stuffing

APPLE

Opening for stuffing

BANANA

Opening for stuffing

STEM

SMALL LEAF

LARGE LEAF

Opening for stuffing

Opening for stuffing

Opening for stuffing

ORANGE

49

Busy Bees in a Hive

This toy encourages your child to discriminate between "same" and "different" and to put together things that are alike. Your child matches the bee color with the color of the pocket: the blue bee goes into the blue pocket. The ability to sort and classify is an important reading-readiness skill. Busy Bees in a Hive also introduces the concepts of "full" and "empty" as your child flies the bees in and out of the hive. In addition, hiding and finding the bees encourages your child to explore the world around her.

MATERIALS

Cotton fabrics:
½ yard 45"-wide yellow
9" × 12" piece red
9" × 12" piece blue
Extra-loft quilt batting:
two 10" × 12" pieces
6½" × 7" piece

¼ yard 36"-wide fusible interfacing
1" strip ¾"-wide Velcro
1 yard six-strand black embroidery floss
Black thread and thread to match fabrics

See How to Enlarge Patterns in General Directions, page 12.

Enlarge and cut pattern pieces from paper. Draw quilting lines (broken lines) and mark all dots on hive patterns. Draw eye, mouth, and stripes (broken lines) on bee body.

To construct hive, cut four hive pieces and two hive bottom pieces from yellow fabric. Mark quilting lines with chalk on right side of two hive pieces.

Cut two hive pieces from interfacing. Fuse to unmarked hive pieces.

Place interfaced and marked hive pieces right

sides together, with 10″ × 12″ piece of batting underneath.

Machine-stitch with ¼″ seam, leaving bottom edge unstitched. Trim batting slightly larger than fabric (save batting scraps for stuffing bees). Turn hive pieces right side out. Baste layers together 1″ from outside edge. Starting at bottom of hive pieces, machine-stitch over drawn lines. Start stitching each line from opposite side to prevent puckering.

Zigzag-stitch bottom edge. Trim excess batting.

Mark pocket-placement dots on hive pieces. From red and blue fabrics, cut two pockets each. Cut four pockets from interfacing and fuse to fabric pockets. Press all pocket edges under ¼″. Hem top edge of each pocket.

Pin blue and red pocket to each hive piece. Top pocket edges must be squeezed to create gap to allow bees to be inserted. Topstitch pockets into place with ⅛″ seam. See Diagram A.

With right sides together slipstitch sides of hive between dots, leaving top open.

Sandwich batting between two bottom hive pieces. Pin, then zigzag-stitch along edge of fab-

ric. Trim excess batting.

With right sides together and lining up dots on bottom with side seams of hive, stitch hive sides to hive bottom with ¼″ seam. See Diagram B.

Slipstitch Velcro fasteners to top inside hive.

To construct four bees, cut four wings each from red and blue fabrics. Stitch pairs of wings with ¼″ seam, leaving 1½″ opening along one side for turning. Clip seam allowance. Turn right side out and press. Slipstitch opening closed. Press wings in half.

Cut four bee bodies from yellow fabric.

Following pattern, zigzag-stitch stripes onto bee backs with black thread.

Fold bee bodies along fold line with right sides together. Stitch with ⅛″ seam, leaving 1″ opening for stuffing. Turn right side out and stuff with batting scraps. Slipstitch opening closed.

Place wings on bee backs. Backstitch along fold with matching thread. See Diagram C. Press wings together away from body.

Following pattern diagram, backstitch mouth and cross-stitch eyes onto each bee with black embroidery floss.

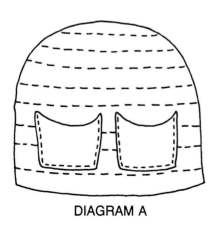

DIAGRAM A

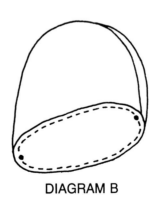

DIAGRAM B

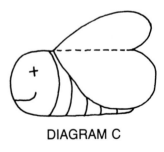

DIAGRAM C

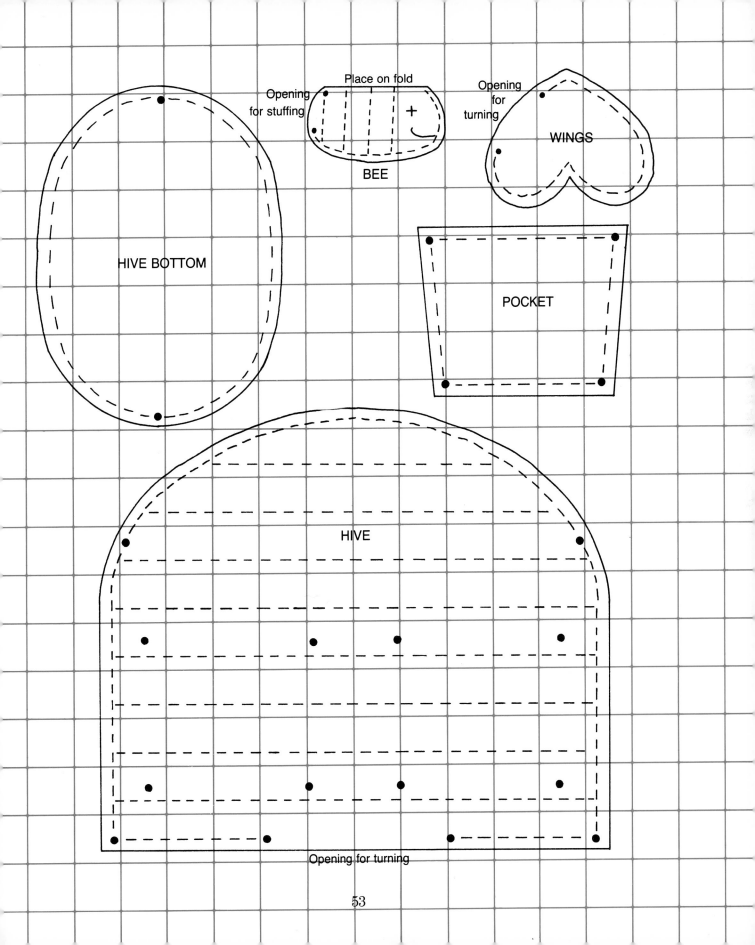

Opening
for stuffing

Place on fold

Opening
for
turning

BEE

WINGS

HIVE BOTTOM

POCKET

HIVE

Opening for turning

53

Pick-a-Petal

Pick-a-Petal is another "all-by-myself" toy. It gives your child an opportunity to develop a sense of order and sequence—an essential skill a child must master before she learns to count or to recite the alphabet.
Your youngster can make choices and direct her actions by removing or adding the Velcro-fastened petals according to her own judgment. Problem solving of this kind helps to develop confidence and self-esteem.

MATERIALS

Cotton fabrics:
7″ × 14″ piece orange
12″ × 14″ piece yellow print
12″ × 14″ piece blue print
Felt fabrics:
1″ × 2″ pieces black and white
1″ × 1″ pieces red, light blue, and yellow

7″ × 14″ piece fusible interfacing
Eight ⅝″ Velcro circles
Few handfuls polyester stuffing
Craft glue
Thread to match fabrics

See How to Enlarge Patterns in General Directions, page 12.

Enlarge and cut patterns A and B from paper. Draw facial features and notches on A. Trace facial features onto another piece of paper and use this drawing as a pattern.

With a hot iron, adhere interfacing to orange fabric. Cut two A pieces from interfaced orange fabric.

On one A piece, slipstitch bottom portion of Velcro circle 1¼″ in from each notch. With right sides together, pin A pieces and machine-stitch around perimeter with a ¼″ seam. Leave 2″ opening. Clip seam allowance and turn right side out.

54

Fill with polyester stuffing and slipstitch opening closed.

Cut out eight B pieces each from both yellow and blue print fabrics. With right sides together, machine-stitch pairs of B pieces with ¼″ seams. Leave 2″ opening. Clip seam allowances and trim excess fabric at points.

Turn petals right side out and press with hot iron. Fill loosely with polyester stuffing and slipstitch opening closed. Slipstitch top portion of Velcro circle ½″ from tip of each petal.

Following traced A pattern, cut facial features from felt, making red mouth, yellow nose, white eyes, blue irises, black eyebrow and pupils. Arrange facial features on A and glue into place.

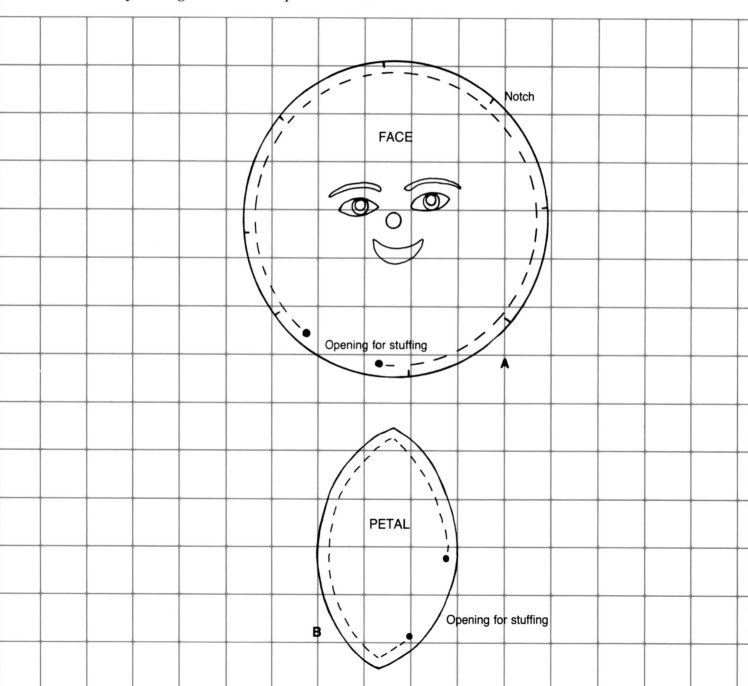

FACE

Notch

Opening for stuffing

A

PETAL

B

Opening for stuffing

Fun Family

*Toy families have always been an important part of
childhood play. Besides helping a child to sort out
relationships among family members, it's just plain fun
to play house. Pretending releases an imaginative
flow of ideas and images.
Both boys and girls will delight in these simple dolls,
and you'll be surprised at how easy they are to make.
Additional clothes can be made in colors other than those
shown here, so that your child can dress up the family in
many different outfits.*

MATERIALS

½ yard 56″-wide, off-white robe velour
Cotton fabrics:
6″ × 12″ piece red
12″ × 13″ piece blue
11″ × 20″ piece red print
12½″ × 16″ piece red-and-white stripe

2½ yards gathered eyelet lace, 1″ wide
Small scrap black felt
28″ elastic, ¼″ wide
Red yarn, approximately 16 yards
8 small snaps
Polyester stuffing
Craft glue
Thread to match fabrics
Six-strand red embroidery floss

See How to Enlarge Patterns in General Directions, page 12.

Enlarge and cut pattern pieces from paper. Letter each pattern. Draw facial features on A and B patterns.

From velour, cut four A pieces and four B pieces. With right sides together machine-stitch pairs of A and B pieces, leaving 2″ opening along one side of each doll. Clip seam allowances and turn dolls right side out. Fill with polyester stuffing and slipstitch opening closed.

Following drawings on A and B patterns, lightly draw a nose and mouth on each doll. Vary each one slightly to change expressions.

See Embroidery Stitches in General Directions, page 14. Backstitch over drawn lines with red embroidery floss.

Cut eyes for each doll from black felt and glue into place.

Following diagrams A and B, loop red yarn back and forth across each doll's head, then backstitch into place by stitching along seam line. Use about 2 yards for brother, 3 yards for daddy, 4½ yards for sister, and 6½ yards for mommy.

To make skirts, cut one C piece from striped fabric for small skirt and one D piece from print fabric for large skirt. Press bottom edges under ¼" and machine-stitch eyelet lace into place. Press, then machine-stitch top edge under ½" to make casing for elastic. Inserting safety pin through end of elastic, work 7" piece of elastic through casing and secure each end with a few stitches. Stitch skirt side seam closed.

To make pants, cut two F pieces from blue fabric for large pants. Fold pattern under on cutting line for brother's pants and cut two F pieces from striped fabric for small pants.

Press, then machine-hem bottom edges of pant legs under ¼". With right sides together, stitch one side seam and press seam allowance to one side. Press, then machine-stitch waist under ½" to make casing for elastic. Slip 7" piece of elastic through casing and secure each end with a few stitches. Stitch side seam and inside leg seam closed.

To make large shirts, cut two E pieces from striped fabric. For small shirts, fold pattern under on cutting line and cut two E pieces each from blue and red print fabrics. On each shirt press, then machine-hem bottom edge under ¼". With right sides together, stitch side seams and clip seam allowance on each shirt. Press, then stitch sleeves under ¼". Stitch lace on mommy's and sister's shirts by placing it under the folded edge. Stitch unfolded shoulder seam closed and hem neckline with ⅛" seam. Leave remaining shoulder open, fold each shoulder seam allowance under ¼", and stitch. Stitch a snap at neckline and at sleeve end.

To make bandannas, cut two G pieces from red fabric. Press, then zigzag-stitch edges under ¼". Tie bandanna around daddy's and brother's neck.

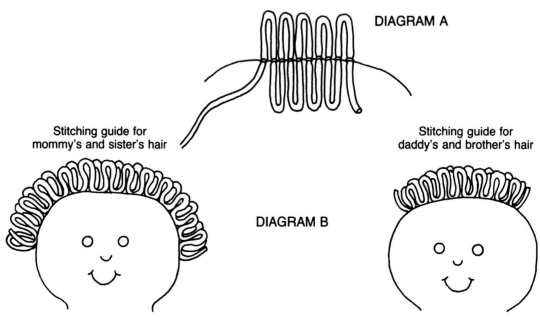

DIAGRAM A

Stitching guide for
mommy's and sister's hair

DIAGRAM B

Stitching guide for
daddy's and brother's hair

58

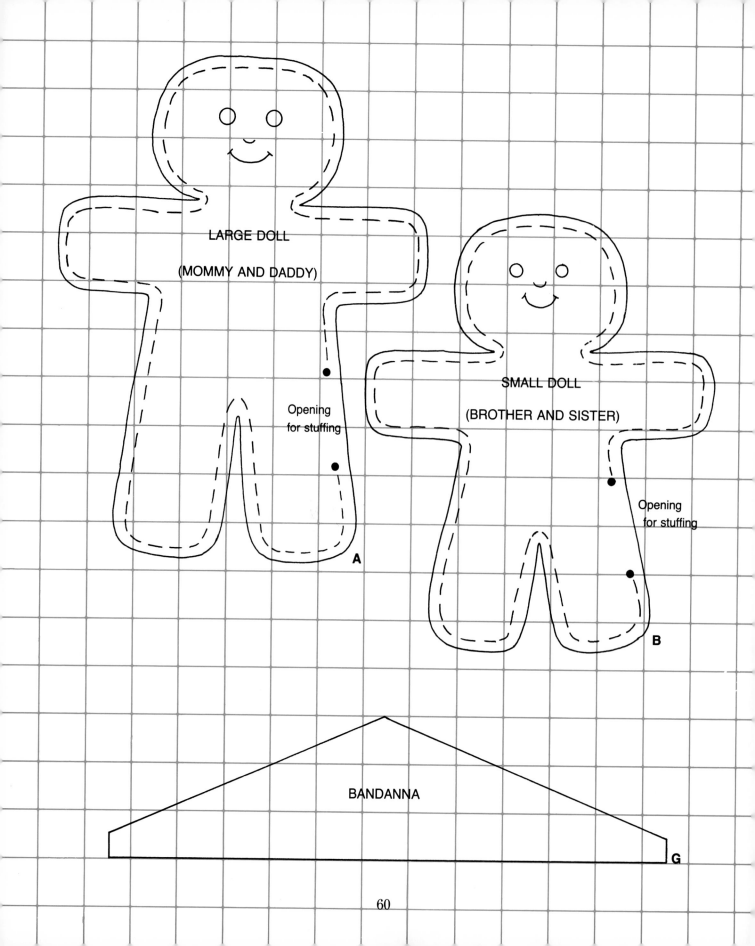

LARGE DOLL

(MOMMY AND DADDY)

SMALL DOLL

(BROTHER AND SISTER)

Opening
for stuffing

Opening
for stuffing

A

B

BANDANNA

G

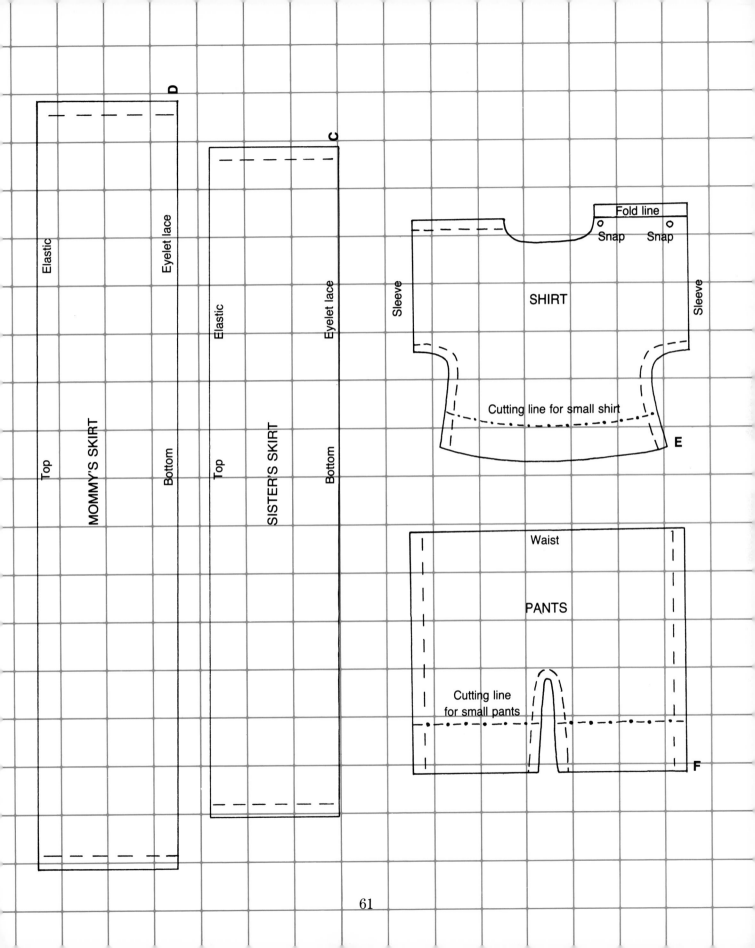

MOMMY'S SKIRT

Elastic

Top

Eyelet lace

Bottom

D

SISTER'S SKIRT

Elastic

Top

Eyelet lace

Bottom

C

Fold line

Snap   Snap

Sleeve

SHIRT

Sleeve

Cutting line for small shirt

E

Waist

PANTS

Cutting line
for small pants

F

61

All Aboard Choo-Choo Train

*The Choo-Choo Train is always a hit with young children.
The cars unhitch and teach a child how to button and
snap. The faces fasten and unfasten with Velcro and can be
moved around, giving your child an opportunity
to make choices as he decides who will be the engineer
and who will be a passenger.
It's an ambitious project to make, but if you take your
time, you and your child will be rewarded.*

MATERIALS

⅜ yard 45″-wide red cotton fabric
Felt fabrics:
8″ × 10″ piece black
6″ × 8″ piece light blue
6″ × 9″ piece pale peach

2″ strip ¾″-wide Velcro
Large snap
¾″ flat button
6 ounces polyester stuffing
2 yards each six-strand black and red
    embroidery floss
Scraps of yellow, red, and black yarn
Thread to match fabrics

See How to Enlarge Patterns in General Directions, page 12.

Enlarge and cut pattern pieces from paper. Letter each train pattern.

From red cotton, cut two each of A, B, and C pieces. From blue felt, cut four windows.

Following pattern, machine-zigzag-stitch windows to right side of one A, B and C piece.

Cut Velcro strip into four ½″ pieces. Center and machine-stitch one side of Velcro to each window.

All seams are ¼″.

With right sides together, stitch A, B, and C pieces, leaving 2″ opening along bottom edges for stuffing. Clip seam allowance. Turn right side out and press.

Following broken lines on pattern, topstitch across couplings on each train piece.

Stitch 1″ horizontal button hole to coupling on left side of C. Stitch button to coupling on B. Stitch snap to coupling on left side of B. Stitch opposite side of snap to coupling on A.

For wheels, cut ten large circles from black felt. Using closely spaced zigzag stitch, stitch pairs of circles. Leave 1″ opening for stuffing. Stuff wheels lightly. Zigzag-stitch opening closed.

Using double thread and stitching through center of each wheel, securely stitch wheels to train.

From remaining blue felt, cut five small circles approximately 1″ in diameter. Center and slipstitch a blue circle to each wheel.

To make faces, cut eight large circles from peach felt. Center and stitch remaining opposite

Velcro sides to four circles to make head backs.

Following Diagram A, draw different faces on each of the remaining four circles.

See Embroidery Stitches in General Directions, page 14.

Using satin stitch, fill in eyes with black embroidery floss. Backstitch eyelashes and eyebrows with black floss. Backstitch noses and mouths with red floss.

To make hair, wind yarn back and forth across wrong side of top edge of front head pieces. Baste into place. See Diagram B.

With wrong sides together and starting at center top edge of head, zigzag-stitch head fronts to head backs. Leave 1″ opening for stuffing. Stuff heads lightly. Zigzag-stitch openings closed. Trim hair to desired length. Attach heads to windows.

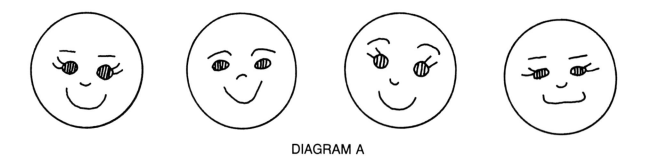

DIAGRAM A

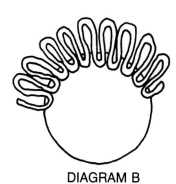

DIAGRAM B

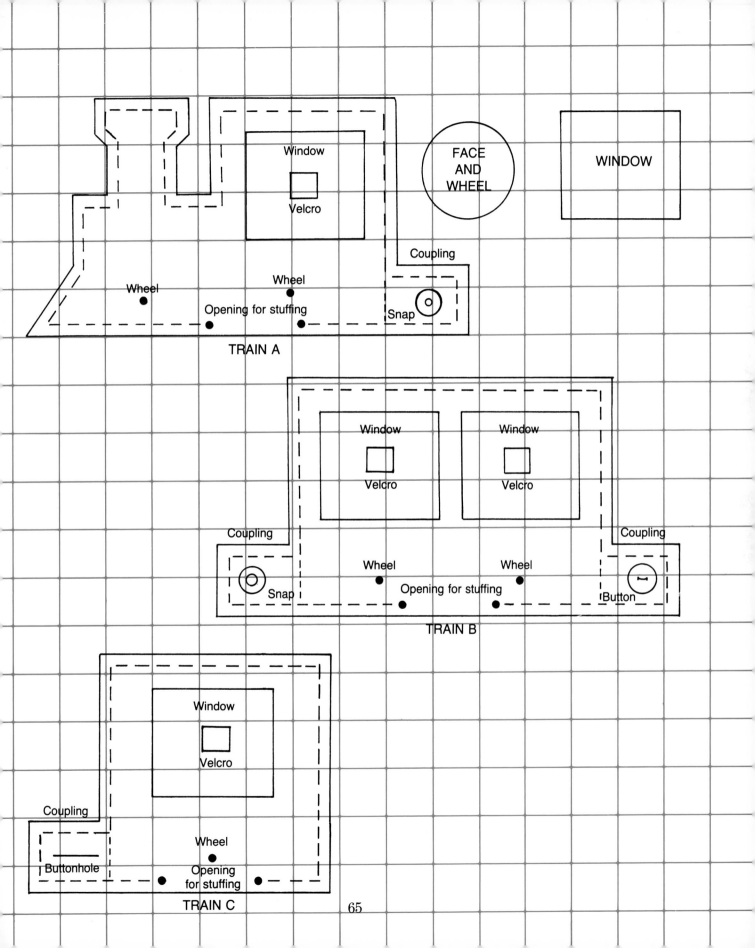

Window

Velcro

FACE
AND
WHEEL

WINDOW

Coupling

Wheel

Wheel

Opening for stuffing

Snap

TRAIN A

Window

Window

Velcro

Velcro

Coupling

Coupling

Snap

Wheel

Opening for stuffing

Wheel

Button

TRAIN B

Window

Velcro

Coupling

Wheel

Buttonhole

Opening
for stuffing

TRAIN C

65

Hoppity Sue and Baby Roo

This pouch-pocket baby and her mommy will help your child to understand the closeness of the mother-child relationship. When your child learns to place Baby Roo in Hoppity's pouch, he will be improving both his manual dexterity and his hand-eye coordination.
Hoppity Sue and Baby Roo are fun, and your child's active imagination will involve them in all sorts of adventures as they scamper together across the nursery floor.

MATERIALS

½ yard 60″-wide fake fur
9″ × 13″ piece pink cotton
12 ounces polyester stuffing
½ yard 3″-wide lace
1½ yards ¼″-wide satin ribbon
4 yards six-strand black embroidery floss
Thread to match fabrics

See How to Enlarge Patterns in General Directions, page 12.

Enlarge and cut pattern pieces from paper. Mark dots, eyes, and noses.

To construct Hoppity Sue, cut one body piece from fake fur with nap running down. Reverse pattern and cut one more body piece. Cut one gusset, one pouch, two tail, and two ear pieces from fake fur.

From pink fabric, cut one pouch and two ear pieces. Mark all dots.

All seams are ¼″.

With right sides together stitch tail, leaving

straight side open. Turn right side out and stuff lightly.

Lining up raw edges, baste tail to right-side seam allowance of one body piece between dots.

With right sides together, stitch head and center back edge of body pieces between A and B dots. Stitch gusset to body front by stitching from point A to 2″ from point B. See Diagram A. Clip seam allowance. Turn right side out and stuff. Slipstitch opening closed.

With right sides together stitch fur pouch to pink pouch, leaving 2½″ opening along bottom edge for turning. Clip corners and turn right side out. Slipstitch opening closed. Slipstitch pouch to body front, squeezing top pocket to fit directly under arms and creating a gap that allows Baby Roo to be inserted. See Diagram B.

With right sides together stitch fur ears to pink ears, leaving straight side open. Turn right side out. Fold raw edges under ⅛″. Slipstitch opening closed. Following Diagram C, stitch ½″ pleat on bottom edge of ear.

Following pattern for placement, slipstitch ears onto Hoppity Sue's head.

See Embroidery Stitches in General Directions, page 14.

Using six strands of six-strand black floss, and following pattern, satin-stitch eyes and nose onto Hoppity Sue's face.

To construct hat, gather top edge of lace. Stitch ends together, forming a circle. Cut 10″ piece of satin ribbon and tie into a bow. Slipstitch bow to top center hat. Cut and stitch remaining 26″ piece of ribbon to underside of hat. See Diagram D.

To construct Baby Roo, cut one body piece from fake fur with nap running down. Reverse pattern and cut one more body piece. Cut two ears each from fur and pink fabric.

With right sides together stitch body pieces, leaving 2½″ opening along back edge. Turn right side out and stuff. Slipstitch opening closed.

For ear construction, follow preceding instructions for Hoppity Sue's ears.

Satin-stitch eyes and nose with black floss. Tie 18″ piece of ribbon into bow around Baby Roo's neck. To secure bow, stitch a few stitches through center knot.

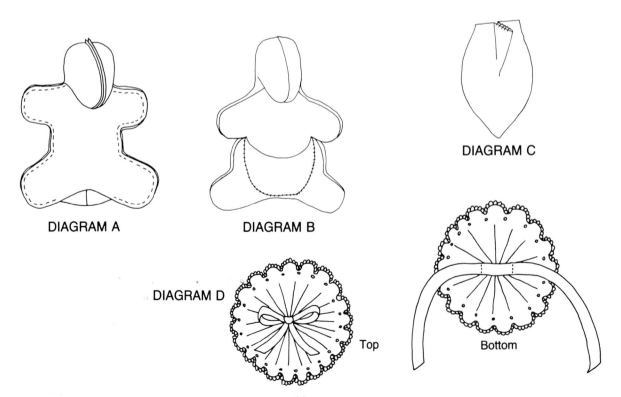

DIAGRAM A

DIAGRAM B

DIAGRAM C

DIAGRAM D

Top

Bottom

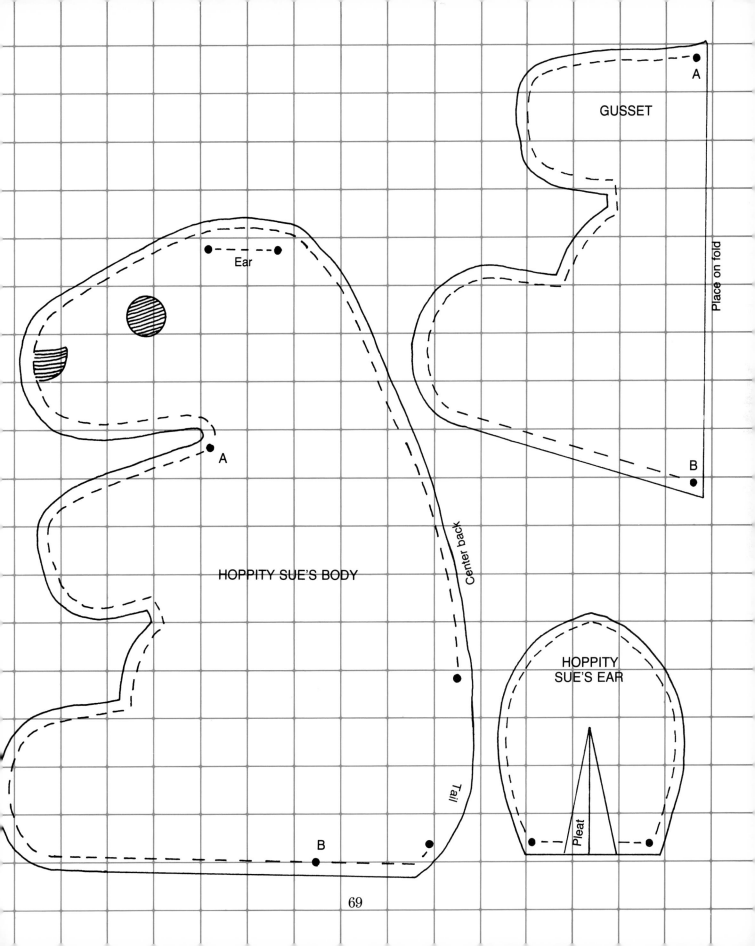

GUSSET

A

Place on fold

B

Ear

A

HOPPITY SUE'S BODY

Center back

Tail

B

HOPPITY SUE'S EAR

Pleat

69

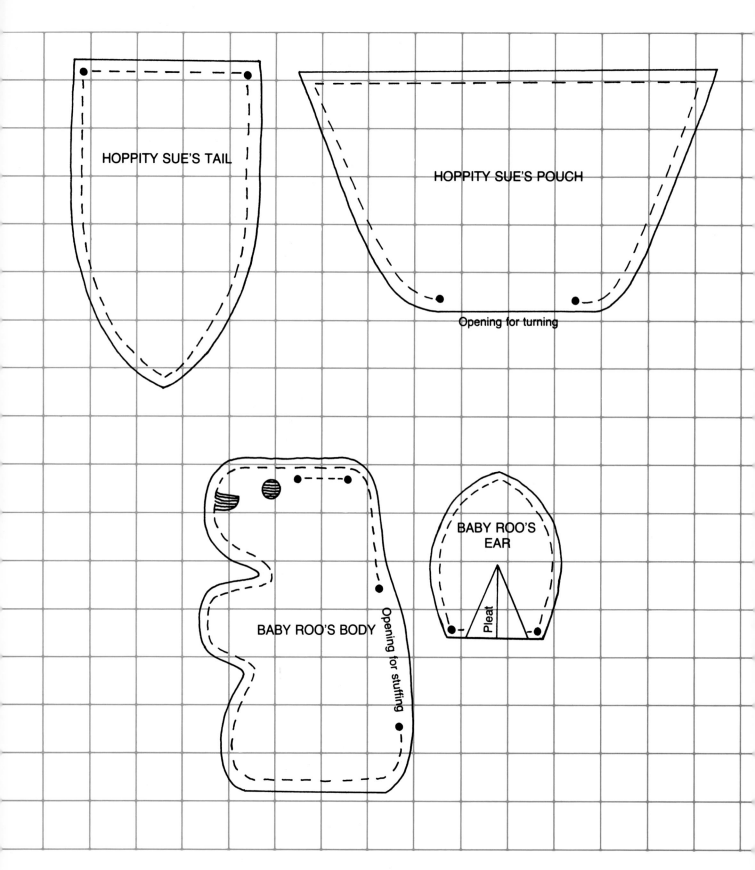

HOPPITY SUE'S TAIL

HOPPITY SUE'S POUCH

Opening for turning

BABY ROO'S BODY

Opening for stuffing

BABY ROO'S EAR

Pleat

70

Sweet Dream Baby with Bunting

*Sweet Dream Baby's arms and legs snap and unsnap—
and your child's manual dexterity is refined and
improved as she practices this skill. She will also learn
the names of different parts of the body and where
they are located.*

*This baby is a wonderful good-night toy. The ritual of
bedtime can be enhanced by putting the baby to sleep in
its bunting. And this lovable doll can teach your child
that there is nothing fearful about going to sleep—not
when you have a Sweet Dream Baby nearby.*

MATERIALS

7″ × 11″ piece off-white robe velour
½ yard 45″-wide cotton print
11″ × 18″ piece quilted fabric
1 yard 1½″-wide lace
⅓ skein (17 grams) super high-bulk brushed
    acrylic yarn
Four #4 snaps
Six-strand black and red embroidery floss
6 ounces polyester stuffing
Thread to match fabrics

See How to Enlarge Patterns in General Directions, page 12.

Enlarge and cut pattern pieces from paper. Draw facial features on face pattern. Mark all dots.

With velour folded double, cut two heads and two pairs of hands. With print fabric folded double, cut two bodies and two pairs each of arms and legs. Mark all dots.

Place head pattern under one fabric head piece and lightly trace face onto right side of fabric with chalk or colored pencil.

See Embroidery Stitches in General Directions, page 14.

Backstitch over eyes with black embroidery floss and over nose with red. Fill in mouth with

red satin stitch.

All seams are ¼″.

With right sides together and lining up raw edges, stitch a head piece to each body piece between dots.

With right sides together stitch doll front to back, leaving a 2″ opening along bottom of body. Clip seam allowance at neck. Turn right side out and stuff. Slipstitch opening closed.

To make each dimple, stitch two ¼″ stitches from back of doll's head through stuffing and out cheek using double thread. Go back to starting point on back of head. Leave thread ends long enough to pull. Tie ends securely, creating dimple indentation.

With right sides together and lining up raw edges, stitch a hand to each arm piece. Stitch arms together, leaving 1½″ opening along one side for stuffing. Clip seam allowance between thumb and forefinger. Turn arm right side out; stuff. Slipstitch opening closed.

Following broken lines on pattern, topstitch fingers on hands.

With right sides together, stitch legs, leaving 1½″ opening along one side. Clip seam allowance.

Turn right side out; stuff. Slipstitch opening closed.

Wrap yarn around 3″ × 18″ piece of stiff paper. Stitch lengthwise through center of strip. Remove paper strip.

Starting at center back of head and stitching over center stitching line, hand-stitch hair to head. See Diagram A.

Following pattern for placement, stitch snaps to body, legs, and arms.

To construct bunting, cut one 11″ × 18″ rectangle from print fabric.

Starting 3″ from bottom edge of quilted fabric, stitch lace to right-side seam allowance. See Diagram B.

With right sides together, stitch print and quilted fabric rectangles with ¼″ seam allowance. Leave bottom edge open. Turn right side out and press lightly.

With right sides facing, fold short sides of rectangle in so lace edges meet at center.

Slipstitch short sides together below lace. Machine-stitch across bottom edge of bunting with ¼″ seam. See Diagram C.

Turn bunting right side out and insert baby.

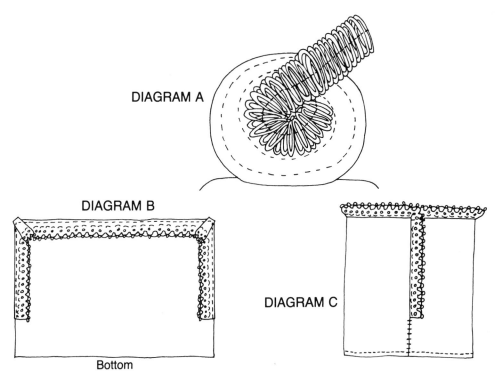

DIAGRAM A

DIAGRAM B

Bottom

DIAGRAM C

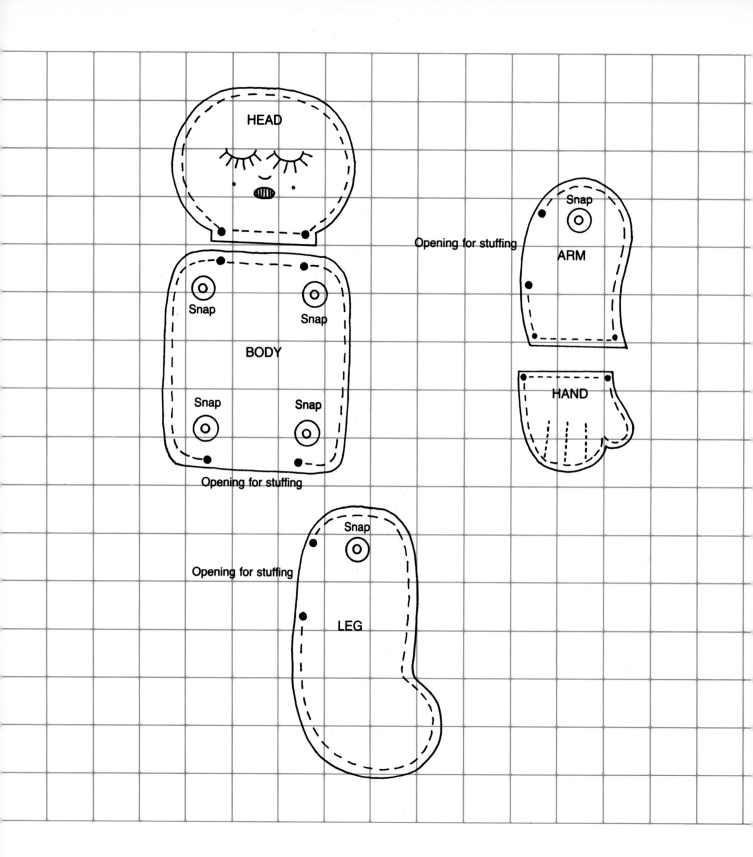

HEAD

Opening for stuffing

Snap

ARM

Snap   Snap

HAND

BODY

Snap   Snap

Opening for stuffing

Snap

Opening for stuffing

LEG

Basic Shapes Cat and Kittens

This toy teaches shape and color identification. A child's interest is held by sorting and classifying shapes and colors that go together, thereby developing the concept of same and different. Basic Shapes Cat and Kittens is sturdy, fun, and easy to make.

MATERIALS

Cotton fabrics:

½ yard blue-and-white stripes
9″ × 10″ piece each of blue and red
10″ × 12″ piece each of yellow and green
9″ × 14″ piece white

Felt fabrics:

Small scraps of dark pink, green, black

12″ × 13″ piece fusible interfacing
10 ounces polyester fiberfill
1¾ yards ⅝″-wide trim
Six-strand dark-pink embroidery floss
Craft glue
Thread to match fabrics

See How to Enlarge Patterns in General Directions, page 12.

Enlarge and cut pattern pieces from paper. Letter each one and draw faces on A and H. Mark top pocket lines on A. Mark dots.

Cut two A, B, and C pieces from striped fabric. With a pin, mark top pocket placement dots on both A pieces.

Cut one D and two D_1's from red fabric, one E and two E_1's from blue fabric, one F and two F_1's from green fabric, and one G and two G_1's from yellow fabric. From fusible interfacing, cut one D, E, F, and G and adhere to the corresponding fabrics with hot iron. Press edges of D, E, and G under ¼″ and baste perimeter of F under ¼″.

From white fabric, cut eight H pieces. All seam allowances are ¼″ unless specified. With right sides together, machine-stitch an H piece to the top of each D_1, E_1, F_1, and G_1 piece. Press seam allowance toward H.

Place pairs of stitched D_1, E_1, F_1, and G_1 pieces right sides together and machine-stitch. Leave 2″ opening for turning and stuffing. Clip curves and turn right side out. Lightly stuff and slipstitch opening closed. With an iron, press and flatten kittens until they are about ½″ thick.

Wrap a 6″ piece of trim around each kitten's neck. Fold one end under and slipstitch closed.

Machine-hem top edge of D, E, and G. Hem F from dot to dot.

Pin D and E to front A piece, and F and G to back A piece. Line up dots on all pocket pieces with pin markings on A pieces. Each pocket opening is larger on top to accommodate kittens. Machine-topstitch the pockets into place ⅛″ from edges, leaving top edge open.

With right sides together machine-stitch C,

leaving the top open. Turn right side out and stuff. Lining up raw edges, center and baste C to bottom seam allowance on back A piece.

With right sides together, machine-stitch B pieces together along center stitching line and press seam open. Line up center seam of B with center bottom notch of the front A piece. Pin, then machine-stitch A to B, easing B around the curves.

Stitch back A piece to joined front A and B pieces, leaving 4″ opening for turning and stuffing. Clip curves and turn right side out. Stuff and slipstitch opening closed.

Place two 15″ pieces of trim side by side and machine-zigzag-stitch together. Wrap around cat's neck; turn one edge under and slipstitch closed.

Following pattern H, cut kittens' eyes and noses from felt and glue into place. Following pattern A, cut cat's eyes and nose from felt and slipstitch into place. Using a backstitch, embroider cat's mouth with dark-pink floss.

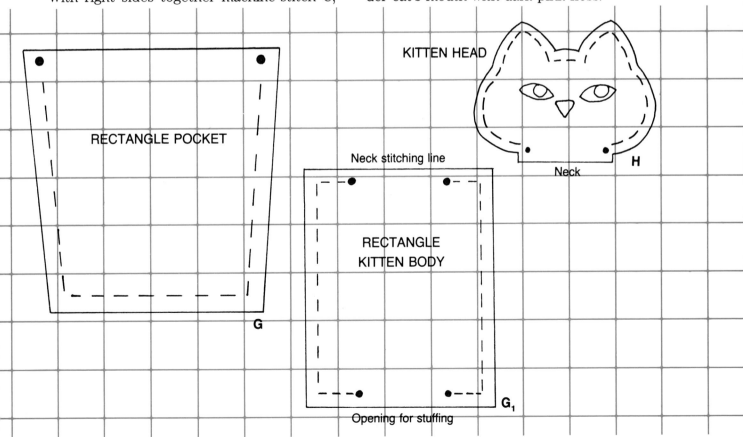

RECTANGLE POCKET

G

KITTEN HEAD

Neck stitching line

RECTANGLE KITTEN BODY

Neck

H

G_1

Opening for stuffing

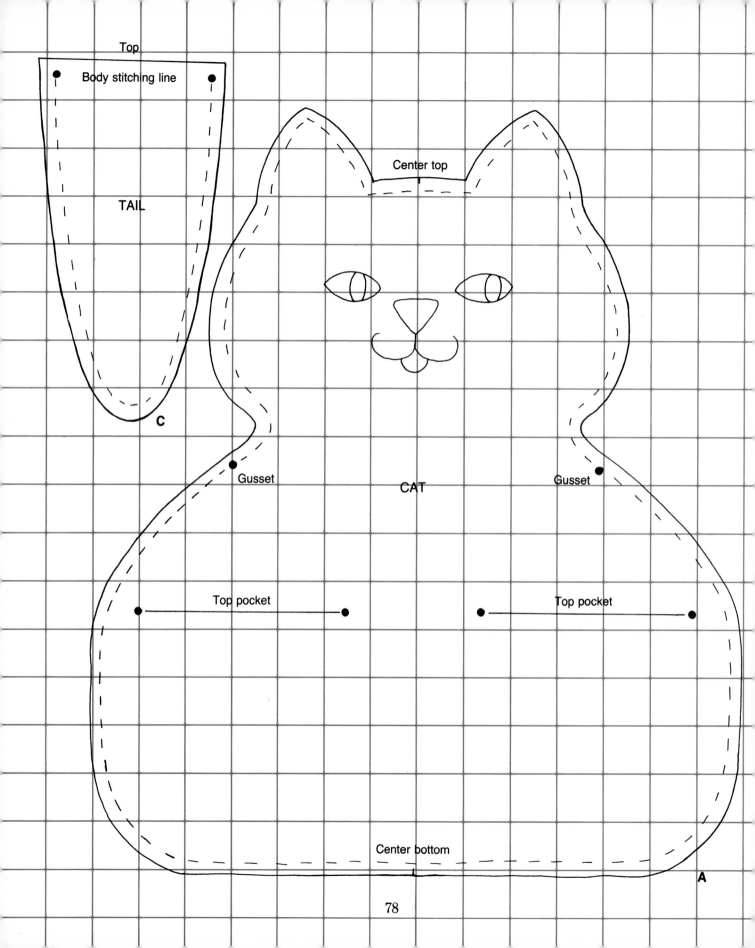

Top

Body stitching line

TAIL

C

Center top

Gusset

CAT

Gusset

Top pocket

Top pocket

Center bottom

A

78

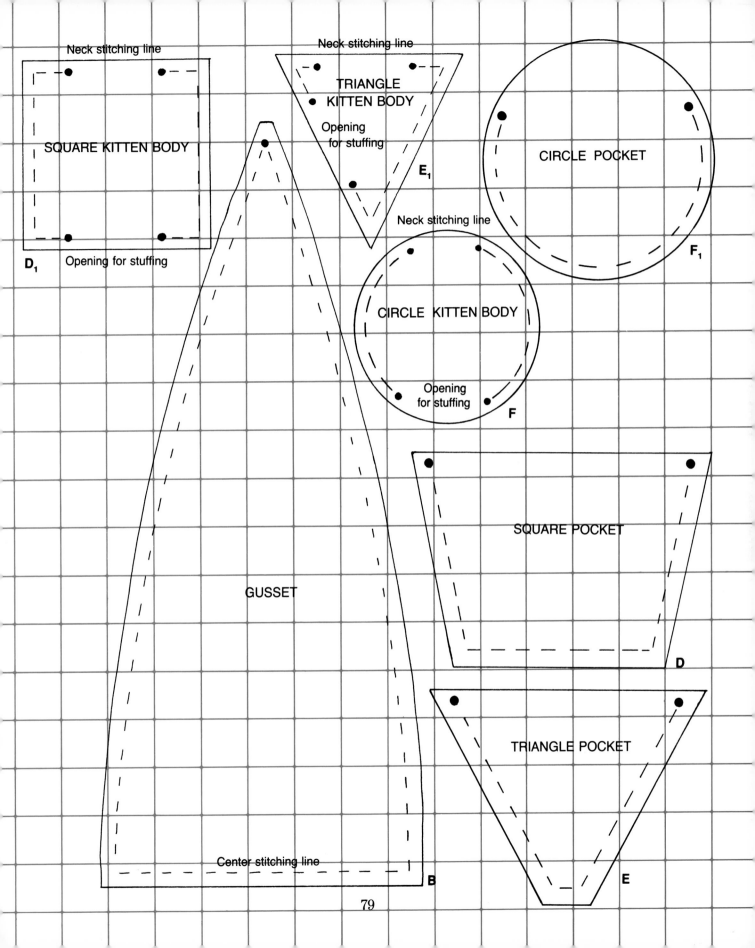

Neck stitching line

SQUARE KITTEN BODY

D₁   Opening for stuffing

Neck stitching line

TRIANGLE
KITTEN BODY

Opening
for stuffing

E₁

CIRCLE POCKET

F₁

Neck stitching line

CIRCLE KITTEN BODY

Opening
for stuffing

F

GUSSET

SQUARE POCKET

D

Center stitching line

B

TRIANGLE POCKET

E

79

Who Lives Here? Rainbow House

Naming and identifying colors is a challenge for young children. Rainbow House is a bright and cheery way to learn about colors, sorting (same and different), and making choices.
Your child will enjoy giving the brightly colored figures personalities of their own and moving them from pocket to pocket.

MATERIALS

Cotton fabrics:
⅜ yard 45″-wide white-and-red print for house
11″ × 18″ pieces red, blue, yellow, and green
10″ × 15″ piece fusible interfacing
2½″ × 2½″ piece black felt
Polyester stuffing
Six-strand black embroidery floss
Thread to match fabrics
Craft glue

See How to Enlarge Patterns in General Directions, page 12.

Enlarge pattern pieces and cut from paper. Letter each pattern. Draw face and bow tie on D and pocket placement lines on A.

From fabric for house, cut two A pieces. Fold A pattern on fold line to make square (A_1). Cut three squares from remaining house fabric. Mark four corners of the pocket placement with pins or pencil dots on two A pieces and two squares (A_1's).

Cut one B, one C, and two D's each from red, blue, yellow, and green fabrics. Cut four C's from fusible interfacing and adhere to fabric C's with hot iron. Press all C edges under ¼″.

Machine-hem top edge of C pieces. Lining up four corners of C pieces with markings on A pieces, pin, then machine-stitch a C piece to each A piece and two A₁ square pieces. Top edge of C will be slightly larger than markings on A. Push in sides of C to create gap for insertion of dolls.

All seams are ¼″.

Machine-stitch B pieces together lengthwise in following order: green, red, blue, and yellow. Press all seams open. Trim ¼″ from outside edge of green and yellow pieces.

Fold B pieces in half and clip seam allowance of green and yellow pieces on fold. With right sides together pin, then machine-stitch joined B piece to A pieces. Line up green and yellow center clips with center top of A pieces. See Diagram A.

With right sides together, pin square (A₁) pieces to sides of house. A will be ¼″ longer than A₁. Start machine-stitching side seam of each square ¼″ up from bottom edge of A₁. See Diagram B.

Pin, then machine-stitch remaining square (A₁) piece to bottom of house. Leave 4″ opening along one side. Turn house right side out and fill with polyester stuffing. Slipstitch opening closed.

To make dolls, place D pieces right sides together and machine-stitch, leaving 2½″ opening along one side. Clip seam allowances. Turn right side out and press with hot iron. Fill with polyester stuffing and slipstitch opening closed.

Following drawing on D pattern, cut eyes and bow tie from black felt for each doll. Glue into place.

See Embroidery Stitches in General Directions, page 14.

Lightly draw nose and mouth on each doll and backstitch over drawing with black embroidery floss.

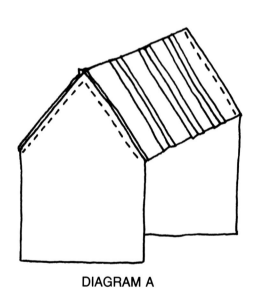

DIAGRAM A

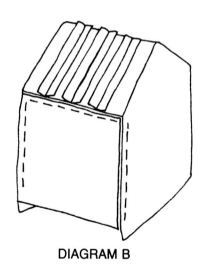

DIAGRAM B

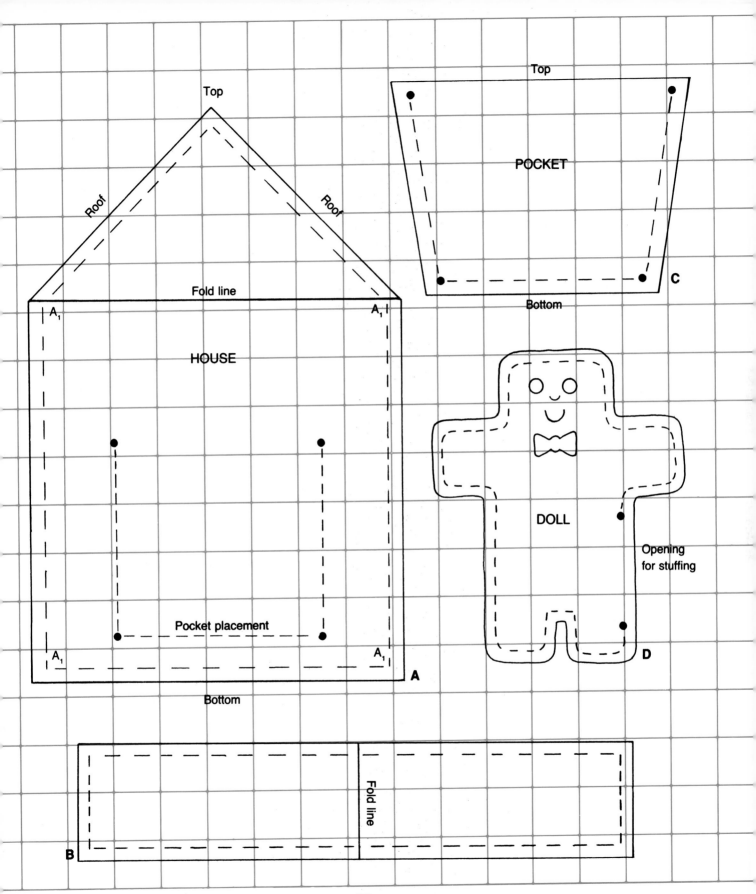

Top

Roof   Roof

Fold line

A₁   A₁

POCKET

Top

HOUSE

C

Bottom

DOLL

Pocket placement

A₁   A₁

A

Bottom

Opening
for stuffing

D

B

Fold line

83

Teach-Me-Shapes Necklace

An up-to-date version of bead stringing, this toy teaches shapes and colors. Manual dexterity and coordination are improved by stringing the shapes onto the necklace. The necklace fastens together with Velcro, so it can be worn for dress-up play.

MATERIALS

Cotton fabrics:
8″ × 10″ pieces red, blue, yellow, and green
2½″ × 30″ piece red

4 ounces polyester stuffing
⅝″ Velcro circle
Thread to match fabrics

Trace pattern pieces. Cut from paper.

With fabric folded double, trace two different pairs of shapes onto each 8″ × 10″ fabric piece. Leave ½″ between shapes.

Add ¼″ seam allowance all around and cut out shapes. Machine-stitch over drawn line, leav-ing 1″ opening for turning. Turn shapes right side out.

Following broken lines on pattern, draw 1″ circle in center of each shape.

With closely spaced zigzag stitch and match-ing thread, stitch over drawn circles. Carefully cut out center of circles.

Using knitting needle or blunt pointed object, stuff each shape. Slipstitch openings closed.

Press short ends of 2½″ × 30″ fabric strip under ¼″. Fold strip in half lengthwise and stitch with ¼″ seam. Insert safety pin through one end of fabric and push through strip, turning fabric right side out. Press. Slipstitch strip ends closed. Slipstitch Velcro circle to each end of strip.

85

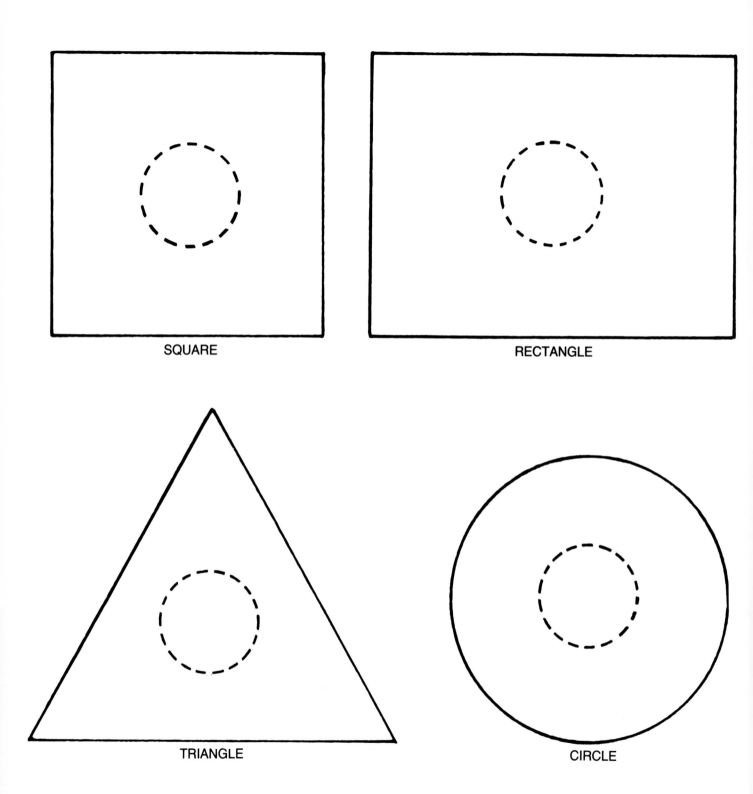

SQUARE

RECTANGLE

TRIANGLE

CIRCLE

FULL SIZE — DO NOT ENLARGE

Teach-Me-Colors Book

This is a good way to prepare your child for reading readiness. Your child will learn to name and identify the objects in the book and will soon be able to distinguish the primary and secondary colors. The Teach-Me-Colors Book will keep your child's interest for a long time, and it's just the right size for small hands.

MATERIALS

Cotton fabrics:

¼ yard 45″-wide white poplin

5″ × 5″ pieces red, orange, yellow, purple, and green

7″ × 7″ piece blue

4½″ × 6½″ piece fusible interfacing

Thread to match fabrics

See How to Enlarge Patterns in General Directions, page 12.

Enlarge and cut pattern pieces from paper.

Cut house from red fabric, ball from orange, flower from yellow, umbrella from purple, tree from green, and shirt from blue. Cut one rainbow piece from each fabric color. From blue, cut 2″ × 7″ binding strip. From white poplin, cut four 6″ × 11″ rectangles. Lining up the short sides, press each rectangle in half to make four double-sided pages.

To make rainbow for title page, place rainbow pieces overlapping ¼″ on fusible interfacing, with yellow on bottom, in the following order: yellow, orange, red, purple, blue, and green. Fuse strips to interfacing with hot iron. Trim excess interfacing.

Open and lay one page flat. Measuring ¾″ from center fold, pin rainbow to left side. See Diagram A. With closely spaced zigzag stitch, stitch outside edge and all raw edges of strips.

Machine-zigzag-stitch a shape to each page, leaving last page blank. Use white thread in bobbin to prevent stitches from showing through to opposite page. See Diagram B.

Fold each page right sides together with appliqués facing. Stitch top and bottom edge with ¼″ seam. Clip corners, turn pages right side out, and press edges.

With rainbow page on top and blank page on bottom, stitch pages together ¼″ from raw edge to form book. See Diagram C.

See How to Bind Edges in General Directions, page 16.

Using ⅜″ seam, bind raw edge with 2″ × 7″ blue strip.

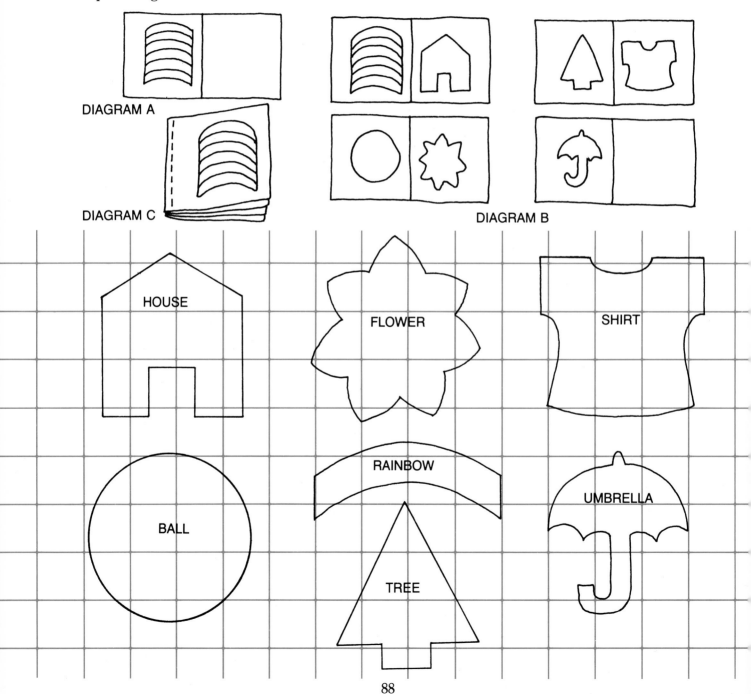

DIAGRAM A

DIAGRAM C

DIAGRAM B

HOUSE

FLOWER

SHIRT

BALL

RAINBOW

TREE

UMBRELLA

Farm Animals

Children have always loved toy farm animals, and your child will find this collection especially endearing because each animal has a distinct personality. With these toys and your help, your child will soon know the familiar barnyard critters by name and the unique sounds made by a pig, a sheep, a chicken, a pony, and a cow. When your youngster pretends he's Old MacDonald, he's on his way to developing a vivid imagination.

Lily Lamb

MATERIALS

10″ × 12″ piece fake lamb fur
2″ × 4″ piece pink cotton fabric
½ yard ⅜″-wide satin ribbon
1 round bell
½ yard each six-strand embroidery floss: pink and black
Few handfuls polyester stuffing
Thread to match fabrics

See How to Enlarge Patterns in General Directions, page 12.

Enlarge pattern pieces, mark dots, and cut from paper.

From fake fur, cut one lamb's body. Reverse pattern and cut one more. Cut one gusset, one tail, and two ears.

From pink fabric, cut two ears. Mark dots with pencil on wrong side of fabric.

All seams are ⅛″.

With right sides together, machine-stitch tail. Turn right side out. Lining up raw edges, baste tail to one side of lamb body.

With right sides together, stitch top body

edge from point A to B. Leave a 2″ opening for stuffing.

Place right-side gusset together with right-side body pieces and stitch from point A to B.

Clip seam allowance between legs, then turn right side out and stuff. Slipstitch opening closed.

See Embroidery Stitches in General Directions, page 14.

Using black embroidery floss for nose and pink for eyes, satin-stitch features.

With right sides together, stitch a fur ear to a pink ear. Turn right side out and sew to head, making a pleat at the base of each ear.

Slip ribbon through bell. Tie a bow around lamb's neck. Tack ribbon securely to body on both sides of bell and through center knot of bow.

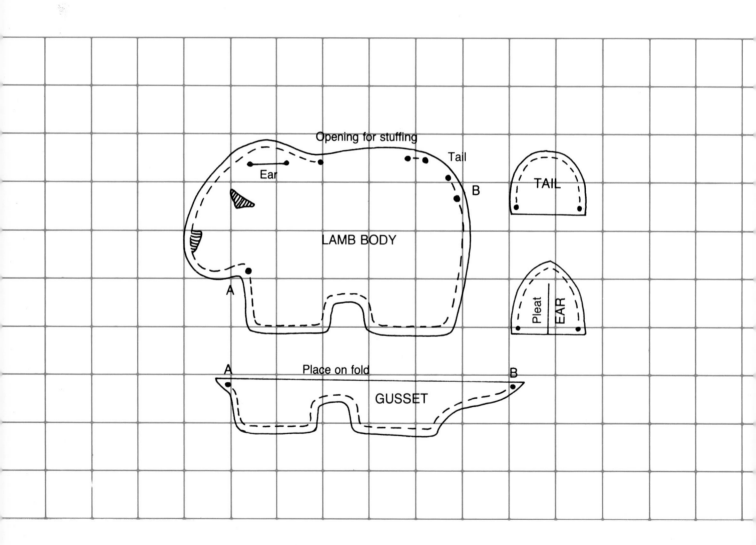

Perky Pig

MATERIALS

9″ × 14″ piece robe velour
6½″ × 10″ piece striped cotton fabric
¼ yard six-strand black embroidery floss
Few handfuls polyester stuffing
Thread to match fabrics

Following preceding instructions for Lily Lamb construction, cut all pig pieces from velour and assemble.

See Embroidery Stitches in General Directions, page 12.

Using black embroidery floss, fill in eyes with satin stitch.

To construct hat, enlarge and cut out all hat pattern pieces. Fold and press band in half lengthwise, then fold raw edges in so these meet at center fold. Machine-stitch short ends together with ⅛″ seam to form a circle. Gather outside edge of hat top. With right sides together and hat top inside band, hand-stitch folded edge of hat band to gathered raw edge of hat top. See Diagram A. Turn hat right side out.

With right sides together, stitch hat brim. Turn right side out and press. Slipstitch brim between band opening and continue stitching around entire band. See Diagram B.

Push walnut-size piece of stuffing inside hat. Using double strand of thread, tack hat securely into place on Perky's head.

Cut out bandanna. Press, then machine-stitch edges under ⅛″ twice. Tie around Perky's neck.

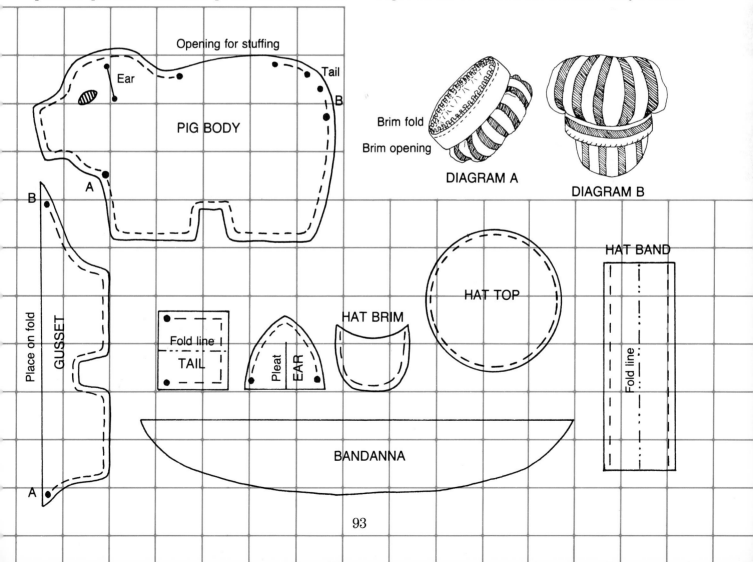

Opening for stuffing

Ear

Tail

B

PIG BODY

A

B

Brim fold

Brim opening

DIAGRAM A

DIAGRAM B

Place on fold

GUSSET

Fold line

TAIL

Pleat

EAR

HAT BRIM

HAT TOP

HAT BAND

Fold line

BANDANNA

A

Carrie Cow

MATERIALS

10″ × 20″ piece cotton print fabric
12″ piece white yarn
½ yard ⅞″-wide lace
¼ yard six-strand black embroidery floss
1 round bell
Polyester stuffing
Thread to match fabric

Following instructions for Lily Lamb construction (see page 90), cut all cow pieces from cotton print fabric and assemble.

To construct tail, press one short side under ¼″. With right sides together, stitch side seam. Insert safety pin through unfolded end and push through tail to turn fabric right side out. Cut four 3″ pieces of yarn. Place these side by side and stitch together in center. Fold yarn in half along stitching line. Push folded end inside folded end of tail. Topstitch tail opening closed along fold. Trim yarn evenly.

See Embroidery Stitches in General Directions, page 14.

Using black embroidery floss, backstitch eyes.

To construct Carrie's hat, cut 10″ piece of lace. Gather along top edge and tack ends together to form small circle. See Diagram A.

Stitching through center opening, slipstitch hat securely to top of Carrie's head.

Wrap remaining 8″ piece of lace around Carrie's neck, crossing one end over the other and stitching along center-front neck seamline.

Using double strand of thread, stitch bell securely into place under Carrie's neck.

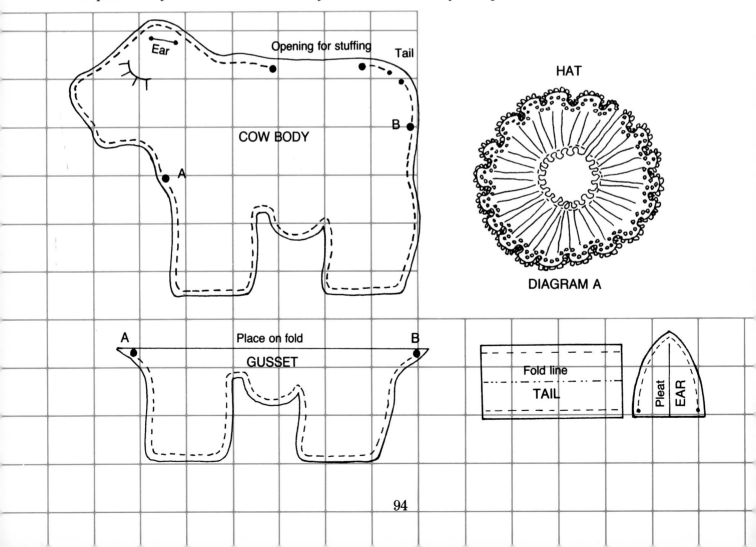

94

Pinstripe Pony

MATERIALS

8″ × 20″ piece striped cotton
2″ × 4½″ piece print
¼ yard six-strand black embroidery floss
4 yards yarn
25″ piece medium rickrack
Few handfuls polyester stuffing
Thread to match fabrics

Following instructions for Lily Lamb construction (see page 90), cut all pony pieces from striped fabric and assemble.

See Embroidery Stitches in General Directions, page 14.

Using black embroidery floss, fill in eyes with satin stitch; backstitch eyelids.

To construct tail, cut six 8″ pieces of yarn.

Stitch yarn strips together through center. Fold yarn on stitched line and baste folded edge to right-side seam allowance of one pony piece.

To construct mane, wrap remaining yarn around 3″ strip of stiff paper. Stitch lengthwise through center of paper. Cut yarn ends and remove paper. Baste mane along center seam line to right-side neck seam allowance of one pony piece. See Diagram A.

To construct blanket, enlarge and cut blanket pattern from paper. Cut one blanket piece from print fabric. Stitch 13″ piece of rickrack around outside edge of blanket. Hand-stitch blanket to pony's back.

For bridle, tack 3″ piece of rickrack around pony's nose. Place 8″ piece of rickrack around pony's neck, tacking ends to underside of rickrack bridle on both sides of nose.

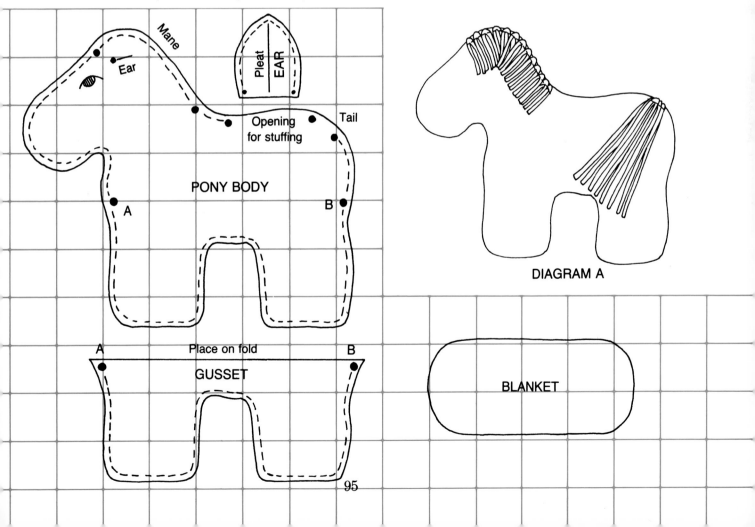

Little Red Hen

MATERIALS

8″ × 10″ piece red-and-white dotted cotton fabric
3″ × 8″ piece white print cotton fabric
3″ × 4″ piece yellow felt
8″ piece ⅜″-wide lace
½ yard ⅜″-wide satin ribbon
Six-strand black embroidery floss
Thread to match fabrics

Trace and cut pattern pieces from paper. Mark dots and draw eye on hen pattern.

From red-and-white dotted fabric, cut one hen. Reverse pattern and cut one more. Cut one gusset.

From felt, cut two feet, one comb, one wattle, and one beak. Baste foot, wattle, and comb to right side of one hen piece. Line up raw edge of fabric with straight edges of felt pieces. Baste remaining foot to remaining hen piece.

All seams are ⅛″.

With right sides together, stitch gusset to one side of hen between A and B dots. Stitch remaining side of hen to gusset, leaving 2″ opening under tail for stuffing. Stitch head and back of hen between A and B dots.

Turn hen right side out and stuff. Slipstitch opening closed.

Following pattern, draw eye on each side of hen's head.

See Embroidery Stitches in General Directions, page 14.

Backstitch eyelashes and fill in eyes with satin stitch. Backstitch beak through center stitching line (broken lines) to hen's face directly above wattle.

To construct apron, with right sides together fold 3″ × 8″ piece of white print fabric in half lengthwise. Stitch side seams with ⅛″ seam allowance. Turn right side out and press. Topstitch lace along folded edge.

Hand-stitch a running stitch through top raw edge of apron. Pull ends of thread to gather apron until edge is 3″ in length. Center and stitch gathered edge to underside of ribbon. See Diagram A.

Place apron around Little Red Hen's neck and tie bow. Tack bow to hen by making a few stitches through center knot.

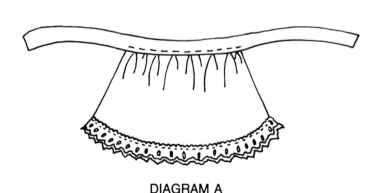

DIAGRAM A

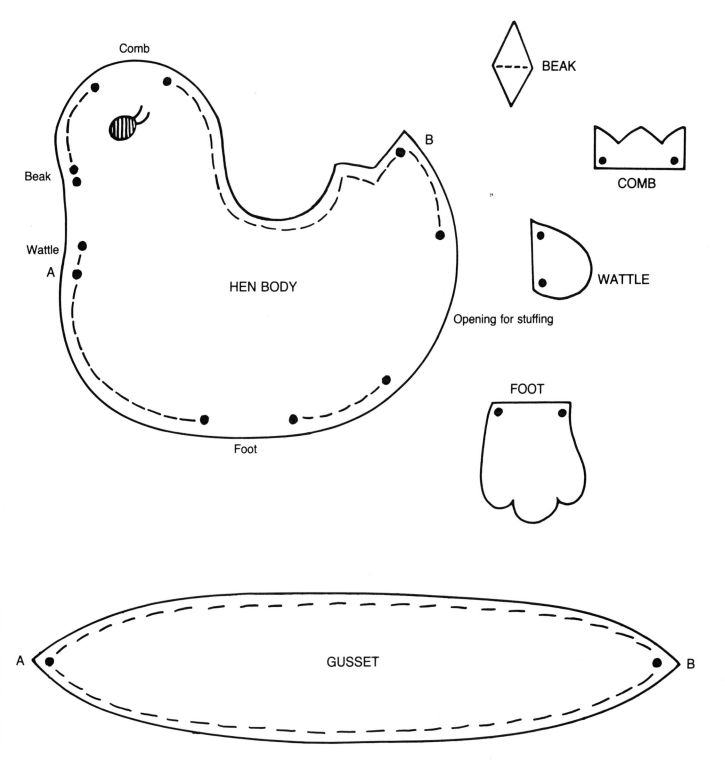

Comb

Beak

Wattle

A

HEN BODY

Foot

B

Opening for stuffing

BEAK

COMB

WATTLE

FOOT

A   GUSSET   B

FULL SIZE—DO NOT ENLARGE

97

Jungle Animals

For indoor fun on a rainy day, round up Jungle Animals and watch your youngster and a friend as they go on safari through towering blocks and across the grassland savanna of your living-room carpet.
Your child will not only learn to recognize and name the jungle animals—zebra, lion, giraffe, elephant, and hippopotamus—but will also develop the ability to move and control objects and to rely on her intuition and judgment in making choices for play.

Zany Zebra

MATERIALS

7″ × 26″ piece black-and-white striped cotton fabric
2″ × 4″ piece black cotton fabric
3½ yards black yarn
Six-strand black embroidery floss
Few handfuls polyester stuffing
Thread to match fabrics

See How to Enlarge Patterns in General Directions, page 12.

Enlarge pattern pieces and cut from paper. Mark dots, eyes, and ear placement.

From striped fabric, cut one zebra. Reverse pattern and cut one more. Cut one gusset, one tail, and two ears. Mark dots, eyes, and ear placement.

From black fabric, cut two ears.

From black yarn, cut six 3″ strips. Stitch strips together through center for tail end.

For zebra mane, wrap remaining yarn around 2″ × 4″ strip of stiff paper. Stitch lengthwise through center of paper. Cut yarn ends and remove paper. See Diagram A.

Stitch mane between dots on right-side seam allowance of one zebra body piece, stitching over stitching line of yarn center.

Press one short side of tail under ¼″. With

98

right sides together, fold tail in half lengthwise. All seams are ⅛″. Stitch tail along long side. Insert safety pin through unfolded end and push through tail to turn fabric right side out.

Fold tail yarn in half along stitching line. Push yarn into folded tail opening. Slipstitch opening closed, securing yarn as you sew. Trim yarn evenly. Lining up raw edges, baste tail to seam allowance of one zebra body piece.

With right sides together stitch top body from point A to B, leaving a 2″ opening for stuffing.

Place right-side gusset together with right-side body pieces. Stitch from point A to B.

Clip seam allowance between legs, turn right side out, and stuff. Slipstitch opening closed.

With right sides together stitch black ear pieces to striped ear pieces, leaving straight side open. Turn right side out. Fold bottom edge of ear opening under ⅛″. Fold ear in half with black on inside. Slipstitch ears to head.

See Embroidery Stitches in General Directions, page 14.

Using black embroidery floss, fill in eyes with satin stitch.

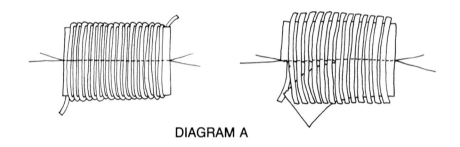

DIAGRAM A

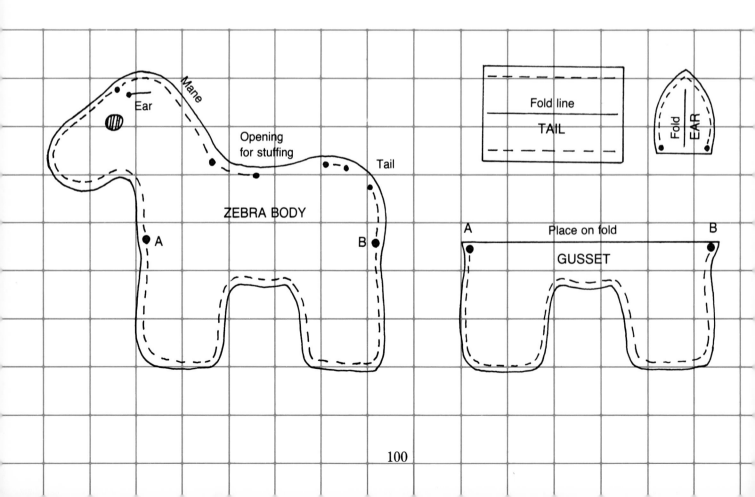

100

Ellie Elephant

MATERIALS

7″ × 32″ piece cotton print fabric
½ yard white yarn for tail
Six-strand black embroidery floss
4 ounces polyester stuffing
Thread to match fabric

Follow preceding instructions for Zany Zebra construction, cutting all elephant pieces from print fabric. Omit mane and do not fold ears.

See Embroidery Stitches in General Directions, page 14.

Using black embroidery floss, fill in eyes with satin stitch; backstitch lashes.

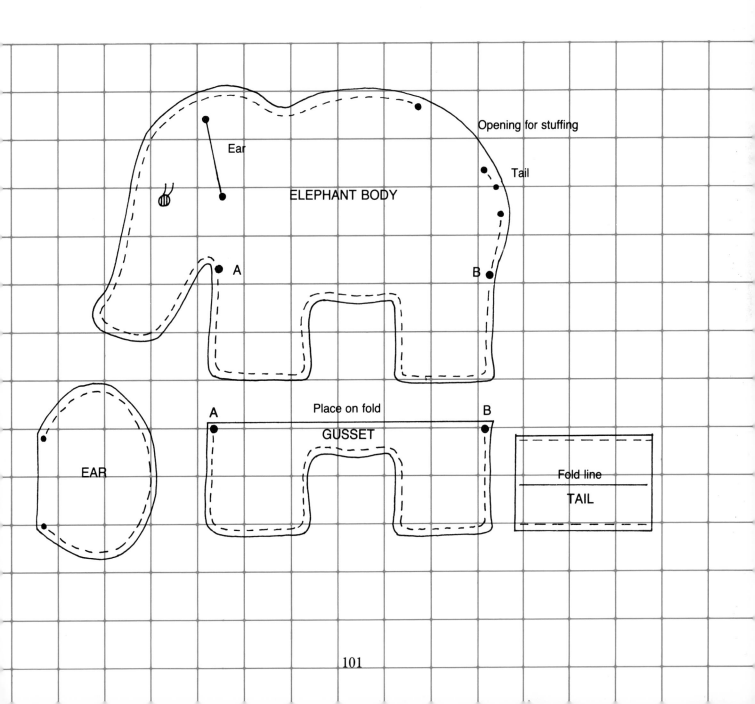

Ear

ELEPHANT BODY

Opening for stuffing

Tail

A

B

EAR

A

Place on fold

GUSSET

B

Fold line

TAIL

Lucky Lion

MATERIALS

6″ × 22″ piece cotton print fabric
2½″ × 4″ piece pink cotton fabric (for ears)
12½ yards yellow yarn
Six-strand black embroidery floss
Few handfuls polyester stuffing
Thread to match fabrics

Follow instructions for Zany Zebra construction on page 98. For mane, cut two six-yard pieces of yarn. Wrap yarn around two 2″ × 10″ strips of stiff paper. Stitch lengthwise through center of paper. Remove paper. Do not cut ends of yarn. Hand-stitch mane around neck of stuffed lion.

See Embroidery Stitches in General Directions, page 14.

Using black embroidery floss, fill in nose and eyes with satin stitch; backstitch lashes.

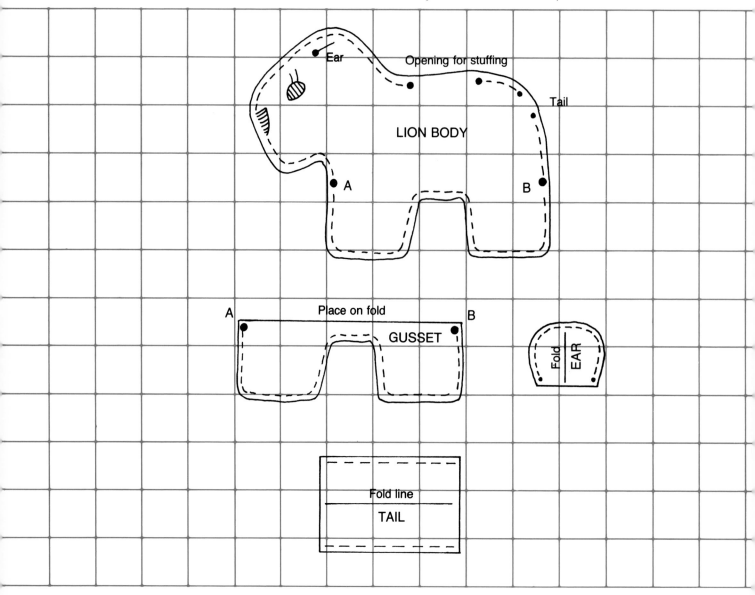

102

Jolly Giraffe

MATERIALS

8″ × 26″ piece cotton print fabric
2½″ × 4″ piece white cotton fabric (for ears)
4½ yards white yarn
Six-strand black embroidery floss
Few handfuls polyester stuffing
Thread to match fabrics

Follow instructions for Zany Zebra construction on page 98. Wrap yarn around 2″ × 5″ strip of stiff paper.

See Embroidery Stitches in General Directions, page 14.

Using black embroidery floss, fill in eyes with satin stitch; backstitch lashes.

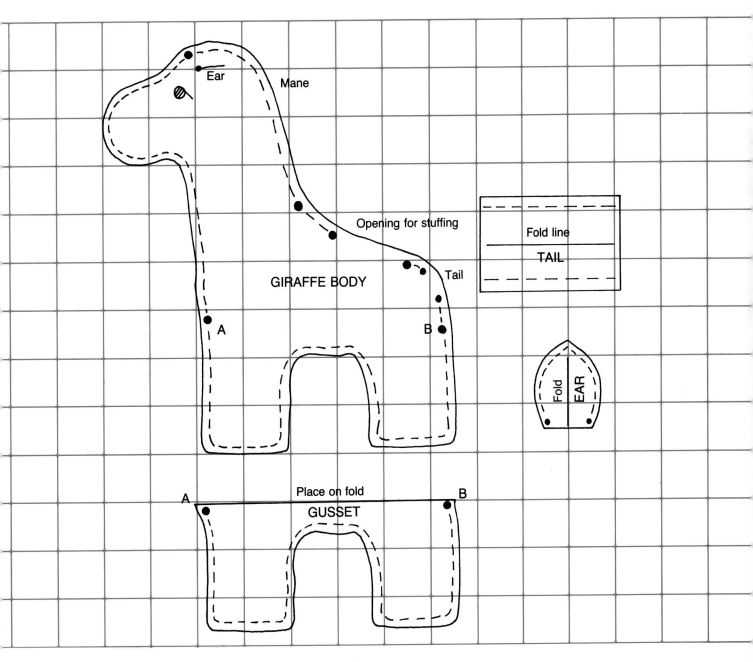

103

Happy Hippo

MATERIALS

9″ × 17″ piece cotton print fabric
2″ × 4″ piece pink cotton fabric (for ears)
Six-strand black embroidery floss
Few handfuls polyester stuffing
Thread to match fabrics

Follow instructions for Zany Zebra construction on page 98.

Omit mane. Cut two tail pieces. With right sides together, stitch tail pieces. Turn right side out and proceed to follow Zany Zebra construction.

See Embroidery Stitches in General Directions, page 14.

Using black embroidery floss, fill in eyes and nostrils with satin stitch; backstitch eye sockets.

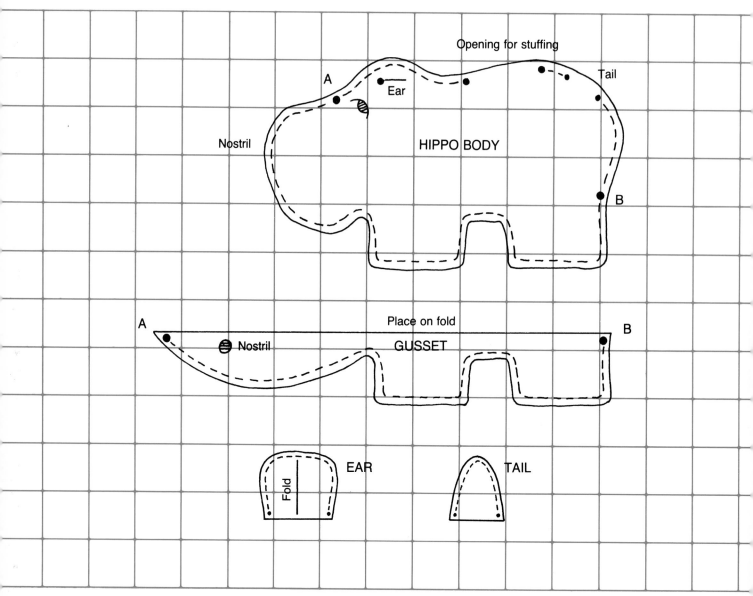

Five Peas in a Pod

This toy teaches counting from one to five. The five peas can be zipped inside the pod, then unzipped to come out: one, two, three, four, five. Your child will never tire of filling and emptying the pod, and he just might get the knack of identifying the numbers in the process. The design of Five Peas in a Pod makes it a perfect toy for long car trips or a carry-along favorite to grandma and grandpa.

MATERIALS

¼ yard green velour, 60″ wide
11″ × 15″ piece yellow cotton fabric
Felt fabrics:
9″ × 12″ piece yellow
3″ × 6″ piece dark pink
3″ × 3″ piece orange

12″ matching green zipper
10″ piece fusible tape
Matching green thread
Six handfuls polyester stuffing

See How to Enlarge Patterns in General Directions, page 12.

Enlarge and cut pattern pieces from paper.

With green velour folded double and nap running down, pin pod pattern to velour. Cut two pod pieces. Cut two pod pieces from yellow cotton, also folded double.

With right sides together, place a yellow pod piece on a green pod piece. With outside of zipper facing green velour, sandwich zipper between the two pieces. Line up one long, straight edge of zipper with top straight edge of fabric. Top of zipper should be 1½″ from stem end of pod. Machine-stitch all three layers together with ¼″ seam allowance. See Diagram B for Banana Babe, page 38.

Turn stitched half of pod right side out to

expose unsewn side of zipper. Stitch remaining pod pieces to this side of zipper to correspond with first pod pieces.

Unzip and turn pod inside out (velour sides together) and machine-stitch around perimeter using ¼″ seam allowance. With machine, zigzag-stitch seam allowance to keep edges from fraying. Turn right side out.

Cut two stems from yellow felt. Place them together and sandwich stem end of pod between center leaves. Pin, then machine-stitch around stem perimeter with a closely placed zigzag stitch. Catch pod as you sew and leave 1″ opening for stuffing. Stuff stem and machine-zigzag-stitch opening closed.

Cut ten peas from green velour. Cut numbers from felt: numbers one and five are dark pink, numbers two and four are yellow, and number three is orange. Center and adhere numbers onto five peas by placing small pieces of fusible tape under them and pressing with hot iron.

To sew peas, place right sides together (numbered and unnumbered sides) and machine-stitch with ¼″ seam allowance, leaving 1½″ opening. Turn peas right side out and stuff. Slipstitch opening closed.

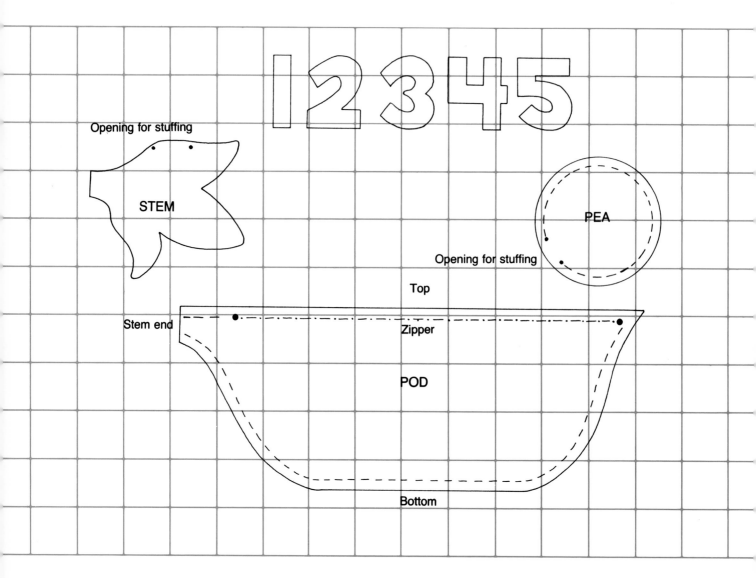

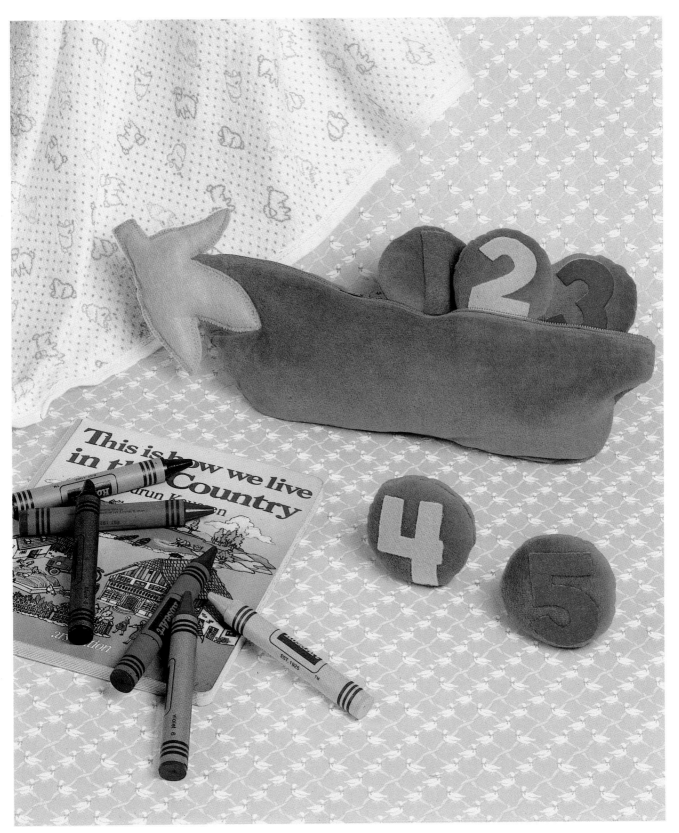

Dino the Dinosaur

*Children become interested in dinosaurs at an early age.
With Dino, your child will learn to tie her scarf with a
simple knot. And you'll be treated to that glow of pride
and satisfaction on her face that comes only with doing
things "all by myself." Dino is also fun for fantasy play.
He's a huggable dinosaur that won't scare anyone.
This is an easy-to-make toy that's a perfect birthday gift.*

MATERIALS
½ yard 60"-wide sweatshirt fleece
5½" × 25" piece print cotton fabric
12 ounces polyester stuffing
2 yards six-strand black embroidery floss
⅝" flat button
Thread to match fabrics

See How to Enlarge Patterns in General Directions, page 12.

Enlarge and cut pattern pieces from paper. Draw eyes and mouth. Mark dots and darts.

From fleece folded double, cut two body pieces, one gusset and two pairs of foot pads.

All seams are ¼".

With right sides together, stitch top body edge between A and B dots. Leave 4" opening on underside of tail for stuffing.

Following pattern, stitch darts in gusset. With right sides together, stitch gusset to bottom body portion. Leave bottom edge of legs open.

With right sides together, stitch foot pads to bottom leg openings.

Turn right side out and stuff. Slipstitch opening closed.

See Embroidery Stitches in General Directions, page 14.

Following pattern for placement, draw eyes and mouth on Dino's head. Fill in eyes with satin stitch. Backstitch eyelashes and mouth.

To make Dino's scarf, cut 5½″ × 20″ strip from print fabric. With right sides together, fold strip in half lengthwise. Stitch raw edges of strip, leaving 2″ opening for turning. Turn strip right side out and press. Slipstitch opening closed. Tie scarf around Dino's neck.

To make hat, cut one hat piece from print fabric. Stitch gathering stitch around outside edge of fabric. Pull thread ends to gather fabric, forming smaller circle. Tie thread ends. Stitching through center top of hat, tack hat to Dino's head. Stitch button to center top of hat securely, covering stitches.

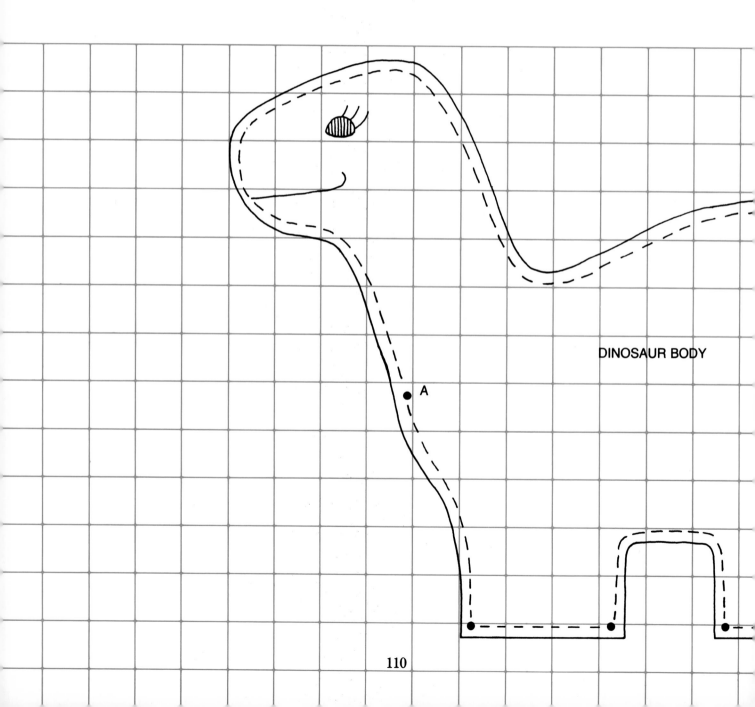

DINOSAUR BODY

A

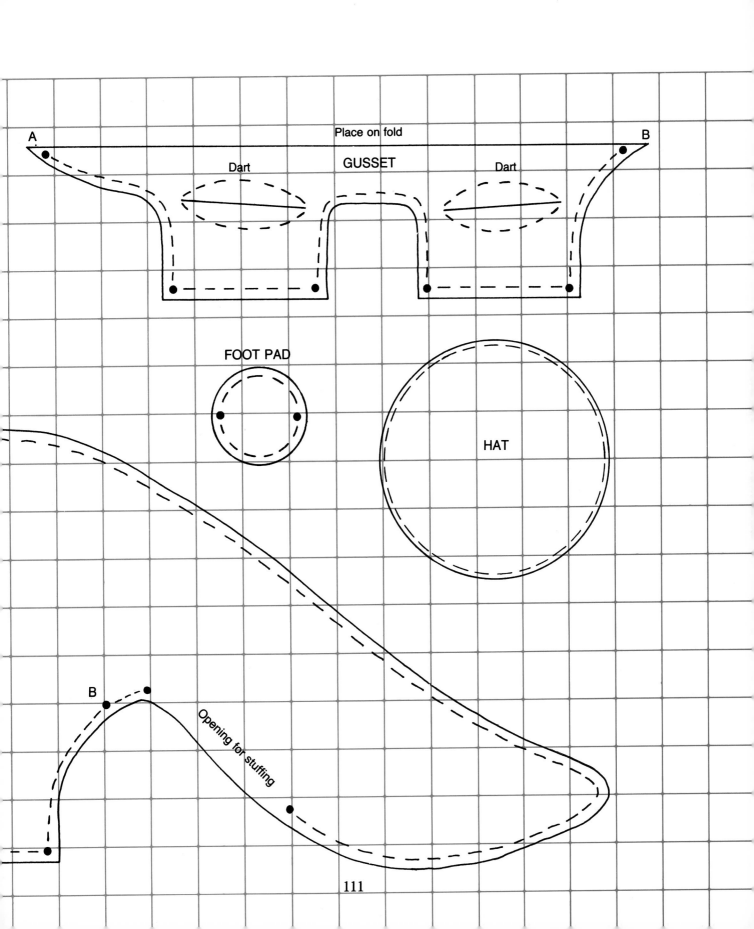

A

Place on fold

B

Dart

GUSSET

Dart

FOOT PAD

HAT

B

Opening for stuffing

111

Mr. Shapey

Mr. Shapey is one of the most appealing projects in this book. Children just love him, probably because he looks so silly and does so much. All the shapes fasten and unfasten with Velcro, so Mr. Shapey provides your child with a range of choices. It's a challenge for a child to sort and classify the shapes and then place them where they belong. And while he's teaching your child her shapes and colors, as well as how to count from one to five, he may well become her good friend. He is an activity toy with a winning personality.

MATERIALS

Cotton fabrics:
½ yard 45″-wide orange
9″ × 20″ piece tan
4″ × 8″ piece yellow (star)
7″ × 7″ piece print (circles)
7″ × 9″ light blue (moons)
6″ × 12″ green (fish)
6″ × 15″ dark pink (hearts)

3″ × 3″ pieces yellow and black felt
12″ Velcro strip ¾″ wide
Polyester stuffing
Craft glue
Thread to match fabrics

See How to Enlarge Patterns in General Directions, page 12.

Enlarge pattern pieces and cut from paper. Letter each pattern. Draw A facial features on separate piece of paper and use as pattern. Mark notches and dots on A.

Cut two A pieces and three B pieces from orange fabric; cut four C and D pieces each from tan fabric.

All seams are ¼″. With right sides together, machine-stitch pairs of C and D pieces, leaving top edges open. Clip seam allowances and turn right side out. Fill with polyester stuffing. Lining up raw edges, baste C and D into place on one A piece (front).

Stitch short sides of B pieces together to form one 48″ strip. Press seam allowances open and one short end under ¼″. Lining up pressed end with bottom center notch of A, pin, then machine-stitch B strip around perimeter of front A piece. When you reach end of B strip, fold edge back so it is flush with pressed fold. Pin, then stitch remaining A piece into place on other side of B strip. Turn right side out and fill with polyester stuffing. Slipstitch folded B ends closed.

Using photograph as color guide, cut facial features from yellow and black felt and glue into place on Mr. Shapey.

Cut two stars from yellow fabric, four circles from print fabric, six moons from blue fabric, eight fish from green fabric, and ten hearts from dark-pink fabric. With right sides together machine-stitch pairs of shapes, leaving 1″ opening. Turn right side out, press, and fill with polyester stuffing. Slipstitch openings closed. Cut a round eye from black felt for each fish and glue into place.

Position shapes onto front of Mr. Shapey and mark each with a pin. Cut Velcro into fifteen equal ¾″ pieces. Slipstitch one half of Velcro pieces into place on pin markings and the other half to backs of shapes.

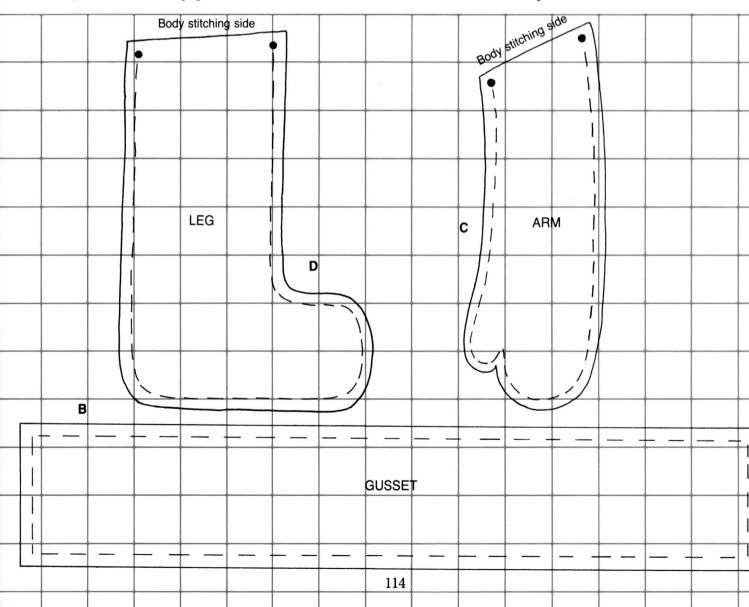

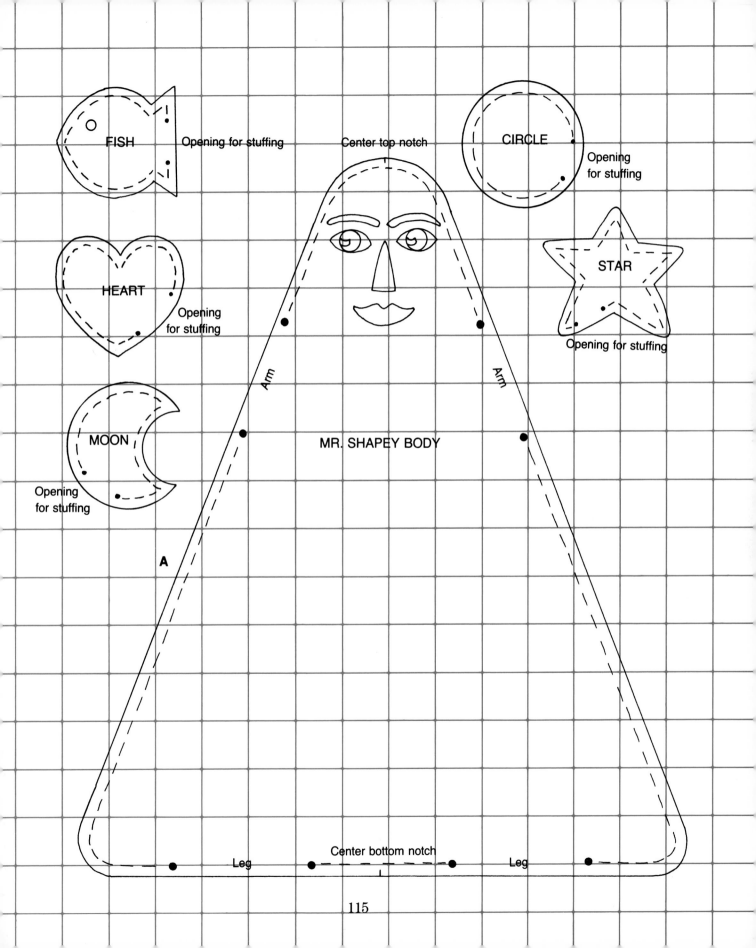

FISH

Opening for stuffing

Center top notch

CIRCLE

Opening for stuffing

HEART

Opening for stuffing

Arm

Arm

STAR

Opening for stuffing

MOON

Opening for stuffing

A

MR. SHAPEY BODY

Leg

Center bottom notch

Leg

Ring Ding Giraffe

*This toy is soft and friendly looking and just the right
size for a youngster to hold. And there's more: Your child
will learn to identify colors and improve his dexterity
by placing the rings on and taking them off the
giraffe's neck.*

MATERIALS

⅓ yard sweatshirt fleece
Three 3½″ × 14″ fabric strips in different colors
12 ounces polyester stuffing
16 yards off-white yarn
Three 1″ pompons
2 yards six-strand black embroidery floss
Thread to match fabrics

See How to Enlarge Patterns in General Directions, page 12.

Enlarge and cut pattern pieces from paper. Mark dots, darts, eyes, nose, and mouth.

With fleece folded double, cut two bodies and one gusset. Cut two pairs of ears and one tail piece. The right-side fabric is the fleece side.

Wrap 15 yards of yarn around 2″ × 9″ strip of paper. Secure ends with tape. Machine-stitch lengthwise along strip ¼″ from edge. Remove paper.

Stitching over yarn stitching line, stitch yarn to right-side seam allowance of one body piece between dots indicating mane position.

Wrap remaining 1 yard of yarn around 2″ strip of paper. Carefully remove paper and baste wrapped yarn to bottom right-side seam allowance of tail piece.

All seams are ¼″.

With right sides together fold tail on fold line and stitch, leaving top edge open. Turn tail right side out. Trim yarn evenly. Lining up raw edges, baste tail top to seam allowance of one body piece between dots.

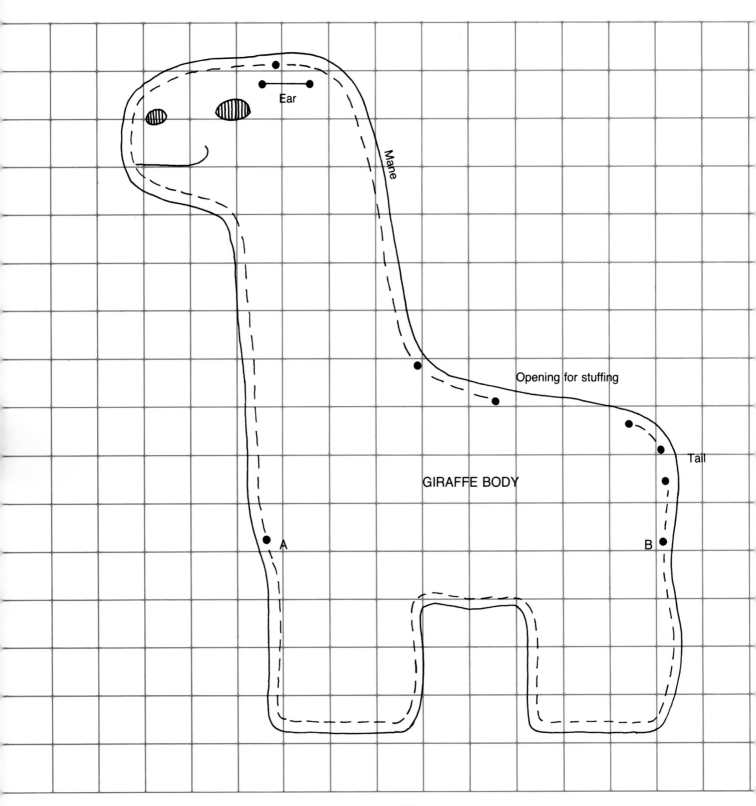

Ear

Mane

Opening for stuffing

GIRAFFE BODY

Tail

A

B

118

With right sides together stitch top of body pieces between A and B dots, leaving 3" opening along back for stuffing.

Following pattern, stitch darts in gusset. Stitch gusset to bottom of body pieces. Turn giraffe right side out and stuff. Slipstitch opening closed.

Trim mane evenly.

Following pattern for placement, draw eyes, nose, and mouth on giraffe. See Embroidery Stitches in General Directions, page 14. Using black floss, fill in eyes and nose with satin stitch. Backstitch mouth.

With right sides together, stitch pieces of ears. Turn right side out. Turn raw edges under ⅛" and slipstitch opening closed. Following pattern, slipstitch ears to giraffe.

To construct rings, press one 3½" side of fabric strip under ¼". With right sides together, fold strips in half lengthwise. Stitch strips, leaving ends open. Insert safety pin through end of fabric strip. Push pin through opening to turn strip right side out.

Using knitting needle or some other blunt pointed object, stuff strip. Insert raw edge of strip end into folded end, forming ring. Slipstitch ring closed.

Spread pompon fibers apart. Stitch through center staple using double thread. Stitch pompon securely to ring at seamline.

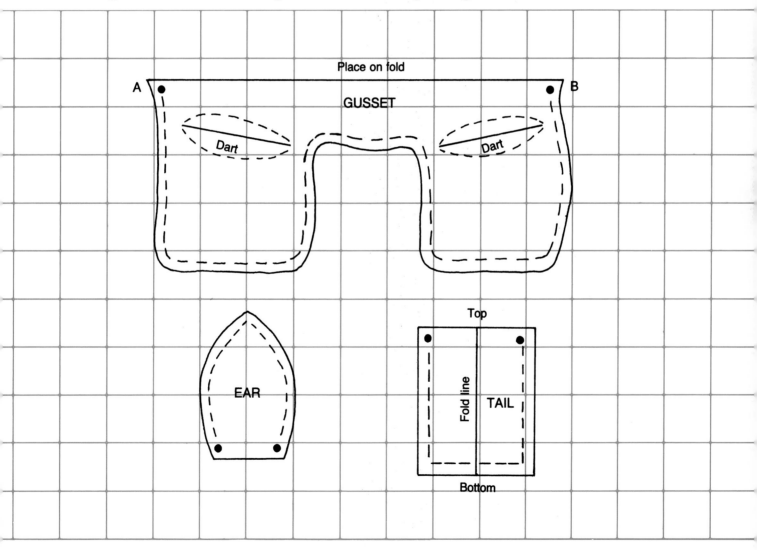

119

1-2-3 Let's Count Book

As baby's first readers, cloth books have always had a special appeal, perhaps because of their softness. This one teaches your child how to count from one to five and to recognize and name shapes.

MATERIALS

¼ yard 45″-wide white poplin
Scraps of six different color cotton fabrics
8″ × 16½″ piece fusible web
12″ × 15″ fusible interfacing
1 yard six-strand black embroidery floss
1¼ yards ¼″-wide satin ribbon
Thread to match fabrics

See How to Enlarge Patterns in General Directions, page 12.

Enlarge and cut pattern pieces from paper. Enlarge and draw numbers and letters on paper.

From white poplin, cut four 7″ × 11″ rectangles. From fusible web and cotton fabrics, cut one kite, two boats and sails, three mice, four mittens, and five birthday presents.

Lining up the short sides, press each rectangle in half with wrong sides together to make four double-sided pages. Open and lay flat.

Following Diagram A, arrange and fuse objects onto three pages. Draw tails extending from mice and kite. With closely spaced zigzag stitch, stitch over raw edges of each shape and drawn tails.

Trace, then zigzag-stitch numbers 1, 2, 3 and 5 onto the upper right-hand corner and number 4 onto the center top of the corresponding pages.

Following Diagram B trace, then zigzag-stitch "1–2–3 Let's Count" onto the title page.

See Embroidery Stitches in General Directions, page 14.

Following pattern for placement, backstitch whiskers and make eyes and noses on mice with French knots.

Cut interfacing into four 5½" × 7" rectangles. Fuse interfacing to one wrong side of each double page.

Divide ribbon into six 8" pieces. Tie each piece into a bow. Stitching through center knot, tack bow to tail of kite and to top of each birthday present.

Fold each page with right sides together. Stitch top and bottom with ¼" seam. Turn pages right side out. Press edges.

Arrange pages in numerical order and stitch together ¼" from raw edge to form book.

Cut 2" × 7½" strip of cotton fabric.

See How to Bind Edges in General Directions, page 16.

Using ¼" seam, bind raw edge with fabric strip.

KITE

SAILBOAT

MOUSE

MITTEN

BIRTHDAY PRESENT

12345 LET'S COUNT

DIAGRAM A

1 2 3 LET'S COUNT

DIAGRAM B

122

Cozy Kitty

*Cozy Kitty is definitely a "love-me" cat that is looking for
a small person to love back.
Your child can learn to dress Kitty, but she probably will
be most valued for the warm, loving feelings she elicits.*

MATERIALS

⅓ yard 60"-wide fake fur
3" × 6" piece pink cotton
⅜ yard 45"-wide cotton print
Small scraps black and white felt
5" × 30" and 4" × 7" pieces eyelet fabric
1 yard six-strand dark-pink embroidery floss
3 yards ⅝"-wide lace
16" piece ¼"-wide elastic
Small snap
2 buttons, ½" in diameter
Polyester stuffing
Thread to match fabrics

See How to Enlarge Patterns in General Directions, page 12.

Enlarge and cut pattern pieces from paper.

With nap running down, trace onto back of fake fur two bodies, one head back, two tails, and two ears. Trace one head front. Reverse pattern and trace one more. Trace two arms and legs each, reverse patterns and trace two more. Mark all dots on fabric. Cut out all traced pieces. Trace and cut out two ears from pink cotton.

All seams are ¼".

With right sides together, stitch tail and pairs of arms and legs. Stitch cotton ears to fur ears. Turn stitched pieces right side out.

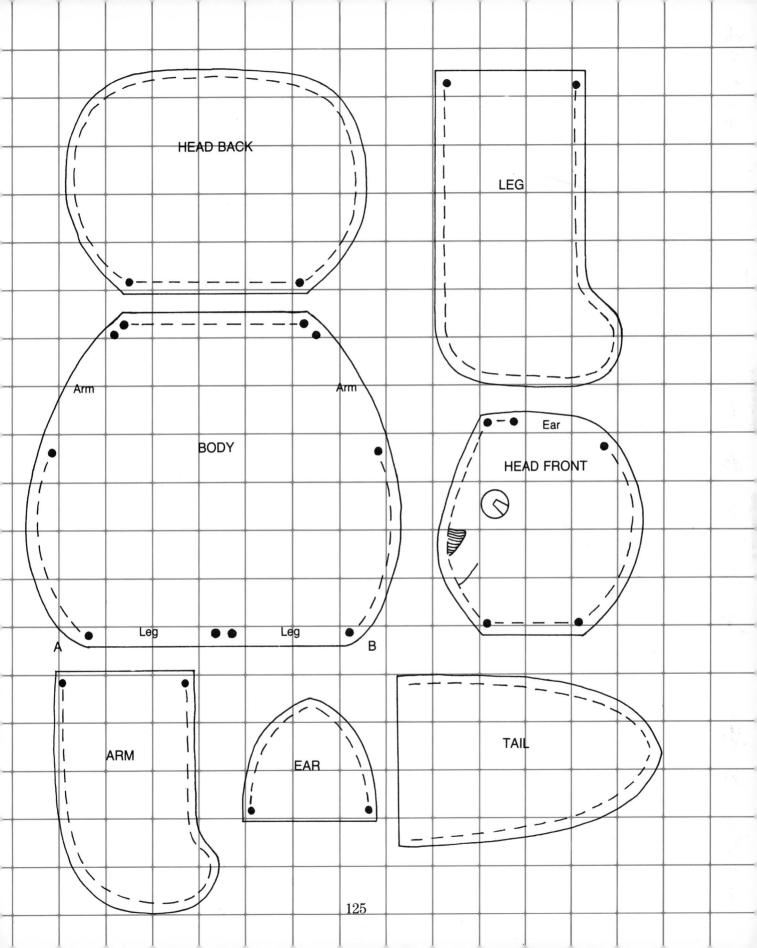

HEAD BACK

LEG

Arm   Arm

BODY

Ear

HEAD FRONT

Leg   Leg

A   B

ARM

EAR

TAIL

125

Lightly stuff tail, legs, and arms. Lining up the raw edges, baste legs and arms to right side of one body piece. Baste tail to center bottom of remaining body piece.

Lining up raw edges, baste ears to right side of head back. Stitch center front head pieces together.

With right sides together, stitch back head to body piece with tail. Stitch front head to body piece with arms and legs. Stitching from A to B, stitch cat front to cat back. Leave bottom portion of body open. See Diagram A. Turn right side out and stuff. Slipstitch opening closed.

See Embroidery Stitches in General Directions, page 14.

Following pattern, satin-stitch nose. Stitch mouth with three large stitches. Cut eyes from black felt and glue white felt highlights into place. Slipstitch eyes to Kitty's head.

For dress, with print fabric folded double, cut two dress fronts, backs, and sleeves.

With right sides together, stitch front center seam. Stitch back center seam below dot.

Press, then stitch right side of center back opening under ¼″. Press left side under ¼″ twice. Stitch. See Diagram B.

Press, then hem neckline and bottom edges of dress under ¼″. Press, then hem lower edge of sleeves under ½″.

With right sides together, stitch dress shoulder seams. Gather top edge of sleeves between dots to fit armholes of dress. With right sides together, pin, then stitch. See Diagram C. Stitch lace to bottom edge of sleeves. Stitch dress side seams. Turn right side out. Stitch lace to bottom edge of dress and around neckline. Sew snap to top-center back opening. Sew buttons to center front. Place dress on Cozy Kitty.

For pinafore press, then stitch one long side of 5″ × 30″ piece of eyelet fabric under ¼″. Stitch top edge under ⅜″ to make casing. Insert safety pin through end of elastic and push through casing. Secure each end to fabric with a few stitches. Stitch side seam.

Divide 4″ × 7″ piece of eyelet fabric into two 2″ × 7″ strips. Press both long sides of each strip under ¼″. Fold and press strips in half lengthwise so folded edges meet. Topstitch each strip along edges to make pinafore straps.

Place pinafore skirt on Cozy Kitty. Position a strap over each shoulder and slipstitch ends to inside top edge of pinafore skirt.

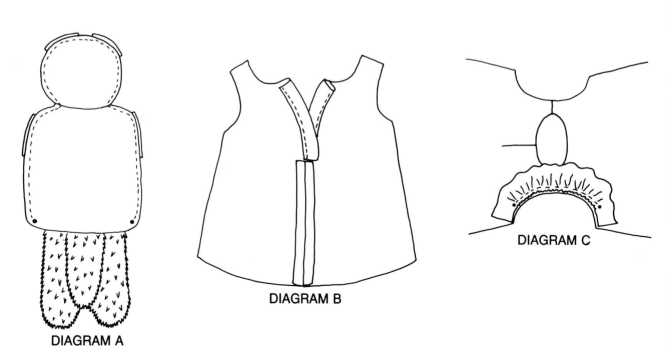

DIAGRAM A

DIAGRAM B

DIAGRAM C

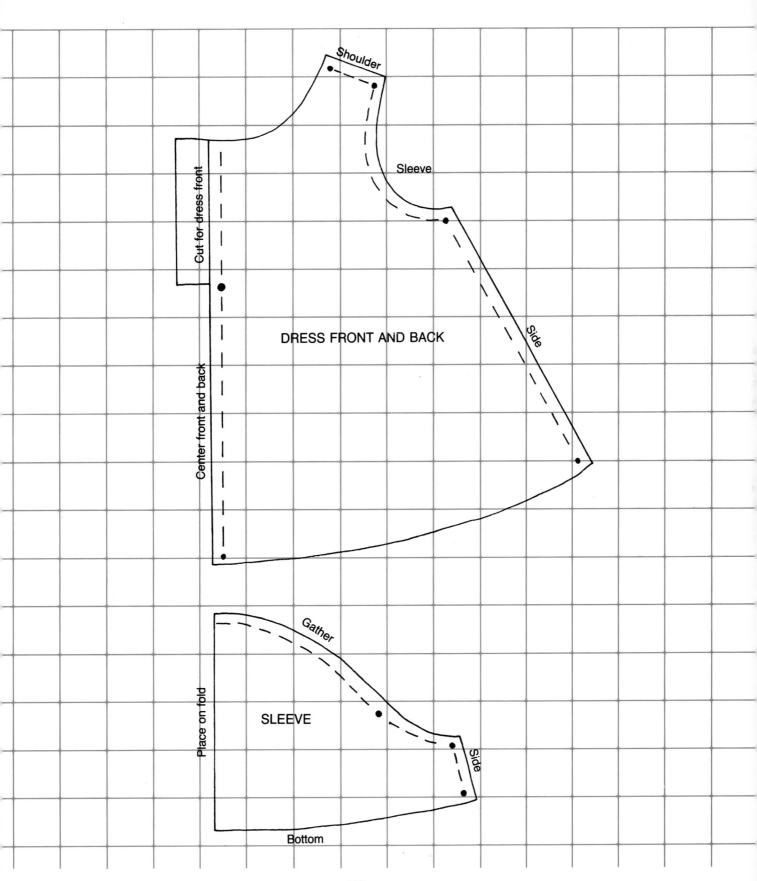

Shoulder

Sleeve

Cut for dress front

DRESS FRONT AND BACK

Side

Center front and back

Gather

Place on fold

SLEEVE

Side

Bottom

Betsy and Bobby Dress-Up

Betsy and Bobby are cloth dolls that your child can spend hours of fun dressing in different outfits. Getting dressed "all by myself" is a tremendous accomplishment for a youngster and gives her a sense of expertise and self-reliance. With their happy, friendly faces, Betsy and Bobby Dress-Up will encourage your child to direct her own actions in play situations.

Betsy and Bobby Dolls

MATERIALS FOR BETSY

¼ yard 45″-wide off-white robe velour

Six-strand embroidery floss, 1 yard each black, green, orange, and red

21 yards (approximately 1½ ounces) brick-colored yarn

8 ounces polyester stuffing

Thread to match fabric

See How to Enlarge Patterns in General Directions, page 12.

Enlarge pattern pieces and cut from paper. Mark all dots. Draw Betsy's face on pattern. Draw Bobby's face on separate piece of paper. Draw

MATERIALS FOR BOBBY

¼ yard 45″-wide off-white robe velour

Six-strand embroidery floss, 1 yard each black, green, orange, and red

18 yards (approximately 1¼ ounces) brick-colored yarn

8 ounces polyester stuffing

Thread to match fabric

fingers on hands.

With velour folded double, cut two pairs of arms and legs for each doll. Cut two body pieces. Trace face onto right-side head of one body piece.

With right sides together, stitch pairs of arms and legs. Leave straight sides open. Clip hand seam allowance between thumb and forefinger. Turn right side out. Fill with polyester stuffing.

Fold top leg opening so seam allowances meet. See Diagram A.

Following pattern, machine-stitch fingers into hands.

Line up raw edges, and baste legs and arms to right side of front body piece. See Diagram B.

With right sides together stitch body pieces, starting at center top of head and stitching to bottom of each body side. Leave bottom edge of body unstitched. See Diagram C.

Clip neck seam allowance. Turn right side out and stuff. Slipstitch opening closed.

See Embroidery Stitches in General Directions, page 14.

Using black floss and backstitch, outline eyes and stitch eyelashes. Using green floss, fill in irises. With black floss, stitch three horizontal lines inside irises to make pupils. Using orange floss, backstitch nose and stitch French knots to make freckles. Using red floss, fill in mouth with satin stitch.

To make each dimple, use double thread to stitch two ¼″ stitches from back of doll's head through stuffing and out cheek. Go back to starting point on back of head. Leave thread ends long enough to pull. Tie ends securely to create dimple indentation.

To make Betsy's hair, wrap 21 yards of yarn around four 4″ × 12″ strips of paper. For Bobby's hair, wrap 18 yards of yarn around three 2″ × 12″ strips of paper.

Machine-stitch lengthwise through each strip. Clip yarn along folded edges and remove paper. Starting at center back of head, backstitch yarn strips around doll's head. Stitch through center stitching line of each strip. See Sweet Dream Baby with Bunting, Diagram A, page 73.

DOLL DIAGRAM A

DOLL DIAGRAM B   DOLL DIAGRAM C

130

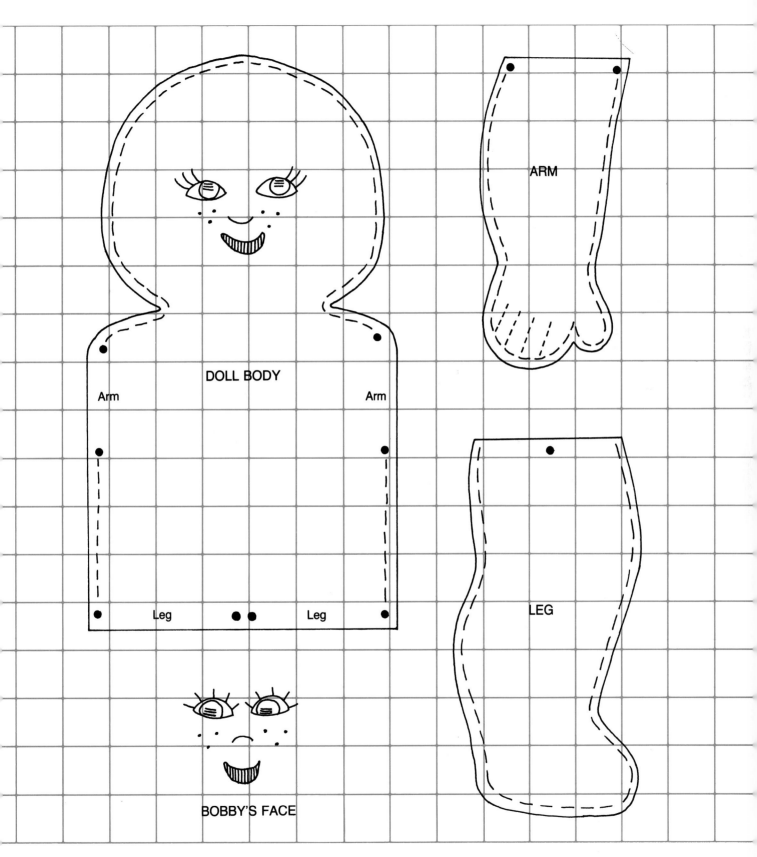

ARM

DOLL BODY

Arm   Arm

Leg   • •   Leg

LEG

BOBBY'S FACE

Bobby's Hat

MATERIALS

9″ × 13″ piece cotton fabric
2″ × 5″ piece fusible interfacing
½ yard single-fold bias seam binding
½″ shank button

See How to Enlarge Patterns in General Directions, page 12.

Enlarge and cut A and B hat pattern pieces from fabric.

Cut two A pieces from fabric and one A piece from interfacing. Adhere interfacing to wrong side of one A piece.

Cut five B pieces from fabric.

All seams are ¼″.

To make hat brim, with right sides together, stitch A pieces. Leave hat stitching side open. Clip seam allowance. Turn right side out and press. Topstitch ⅛″ from fabric edge.

With right sides together, stitch B pieces together along their vertical sides to make hat.

Lining up raw edges, stitch hat brim to hat with ⅛″ seam.

With right sides together, stitch seam binding to bottom edge of hat. Turn binding to inside hat and topstitch around hat bottom ¼″ from edge.

Press hat brim up toward nat top.

Securely stitch button to center top hat.

Betsy's Hat

MATERIALS

7″ × 27″ piece white eyelet fabric
½ yard white double-fold bias seam binding
½ yard ¼″-wide elastic
¾ yard 1⅜″-wide lace
White thread

Press 7″ sides of eyelet fabric under ¼″ twice, then machine-stitch. Press one 27″ side under ⅜″ twice. Press remaining 27″ side under ½″ twice. Machine-stitch both 27″ sides. Stitch lace along edge of ½″ fold, leaving space to insert ¼″-wide elastic between stitching lines.

Cut 6″ piece of elastic. Insert safety pin through elastic end and push through opening of ⅜″ casing. Stitch ends of elastic together.

Push remaining 12″ piece of elastic through ½″ casing. Secure ends of elastic to fabric with a few stitches. See Betsy's Hat Diagram.

Topstitch along edge of bias binding. Cut into two equal pieces. Slipstitch end of binding strips to each side of hat front. Place on Betsy's head and tie bow.

Betsy's and Bobby's Shirts

MATERIALS

¼ yard 45″-wide cotton fabric
3″ × 6″ piece cotton fabric (optional pocket)
4″ × 4″ piece white cotton fabric (optional hanky)
Two small snaps
Thread to match fabrics

See How to Enlarge Patterns in General Directions, page 12.

Enlarge and cut shirt front, back, sleeve, and pocket patterns from paper.

From ¼ yard fabric folded double, cut two shirt back pieces. Cut two sleeve pieces and one front piece. Cut one 1″ × 10″ bias fabric strip. From 3″ × 6″ piece of fabric, cut two pockets.

All seams are ¼″ unless otherwise specified.

With right sides together stitch pocket pieces, leaving top edge open. Turn right side out and press. Fold top raw edges under ¼″ and topstitch with ⅛″ seam. Following pattern diagram, stitch pocket into place on shirt front with ⅛″ seam.

Stitch edges of center shirt back under ¼″. With right sides together, fold center back on fold line and pin.

With right sides together, stitch shirt front to

132

shirt backs along shoulder seams. Press seams open.

With right sides together, stitch bias strip to neckline. See Shirt Diagram. Turn bias strip to inside neckline. Pin raw edge under. Topstitch neckline with ¼" seam.

Press, then hem bottom sleeve edges under ¼" twice. For Betsy's sleeves, gather top edge of sleeves between dots to fit armholes of shirt. With right sides together, pin, then stitch sleeve to armhole.

For Bobby's sleeves, follow preceding step, omitting gathering along top edge of sleeves. With right sides together, stitch shirt side seams. Press, then hem bottom edge of shirt under ¼" twice. Stitch two snaps to center back opening.

To make handkerchief, press, then zigzag-stitch edges of 4" × 4" piece of fabric under ¼".

Betsy's Smock

MATERIALS

¼ yard 45"-wide cotton print fabric
3" × 6" piece cotton fabric for pocket
4" × 4" piece white cotton fabric (optional hanky)
⅔ yard ⅞"-wide lace
2 small snaps
Thread to match fabrics

See How to Enlarge Patterns in General Directions, page 12.

Enlarge and cut smock front, back, sleeve, and pocket patterns from paper.

Follow preceding instructions for shirt. Stitch lace to inside sleeve edge and bottom edge of smock.

Bobby's Trousers and Betsy's Pantaloons

MATERIALS

¼ yard 45"-wide cotton fabric
14" piece ¼"-wide elastic
⅔ yard ⅞"-wide lace (for pantaloons)
Thread to match fabric

See How to Enlarge Patterns in General Directions, page 12.

Enlarge and cut trouser pattern from paper. Cut two trouser pieces from fabric.

Press top edge under ½" twice. Press bottom edge under ¼" twice. Stitch top and bottom edges.

Cut elastic into two equal pieces. Insert safety pin through end of elastic and push through top waistband casing of each trouser piece. Secure ends with a few stitches.

For Betsy's pantaloons, stitch lace to inside bottom edge of pantaloons. With right sides together, stitch center front and back with ¼" seam. Stitch inseam with ¼" seam. Turn right side out.

Betsy's and Bobby's Sunsuits

MATERIALS

¼ yard 45"-wide cotton fabric
Two small snaps
¾ yard ¼"-wide elastic
¾ yard ⅝"-wide eyelet lace (for Betsy's sunsuit)
Thread to match fabric

See How to Enlarge Patterns in General Directions, page 12.

Enlarge and cut sunsuit and bib patterns from paper.

From fabric, cut two sunsuit pieces and one bib piece. Cut two 2" × 7" pieces for straps.

All seams are ¼".

With right sides together, fold bib on fold line. Stitch side seams. Turn right side out and press.

Press one 2" side of straps under ¼". Press both 7" sides of straps under ¼". Fold and press straps in half lengthwise. Topstitch ⅛" from edge.

Press top edge of sunsuit under ¼" and bottom edge under ¾". Hem bottom edge with ½" seam to make casing. For Betsy, stitch eyelet lace along edge of casing.

Cut two 8" pieces of elastic. Insert safety pin through end of elastic and push through casing.

Secure ends of elastic with a few stitches.

With right sides together, stitch center front and back seams. Stitch inseam. Turn right side out.

Center and stitch bottom raw edge of bib ¼" inside front waist. See Sunsuit Diagram.

Stretching elastic as you sew, zigzag-stitch 9" piece of elastic to inside waist. Do not stretch elastic to bib area.

Place sunsuit on doll. Pin, then slipstitch raw edge of straps to inside back waist. Stitch snaps to folded end of straps and top corners of bib.

Betsy's and Bobby's Shoes

MATERIALS FOR ONE PAIR OF SHOES

7" × 10½" piece black vinyl
Thread to match fabric

See How to Enlarge Patterns in General Directions, page 12.

Enlarge and cut shoe top and sole patterns from paper. Cut out crescent shape on shoe top to form strap. Mark dots on pattern pieces.

From vinyl, cut two shoe tops and sole pieces each. With right sides together and lining up dots, stitch shoe tops to soles with ⅛" seam. Stitch back heel seam. Turn shoes right side out.

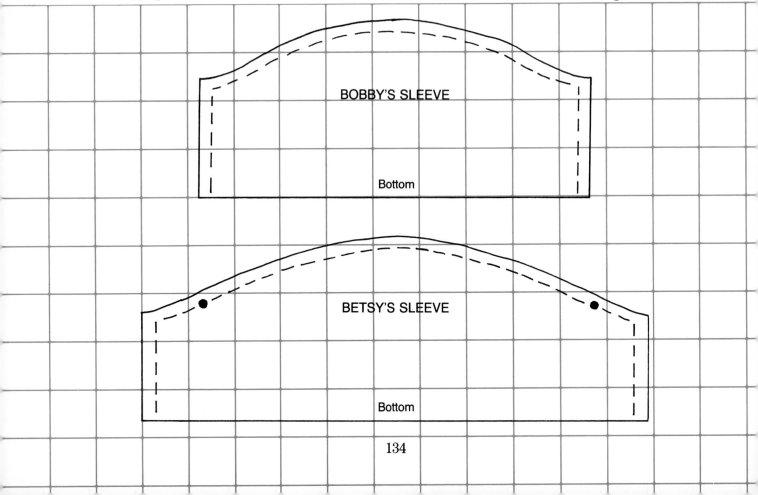

BOBBY'S SLEEVE

Bottom

BETSY'S SLEEVE

Bottom

134

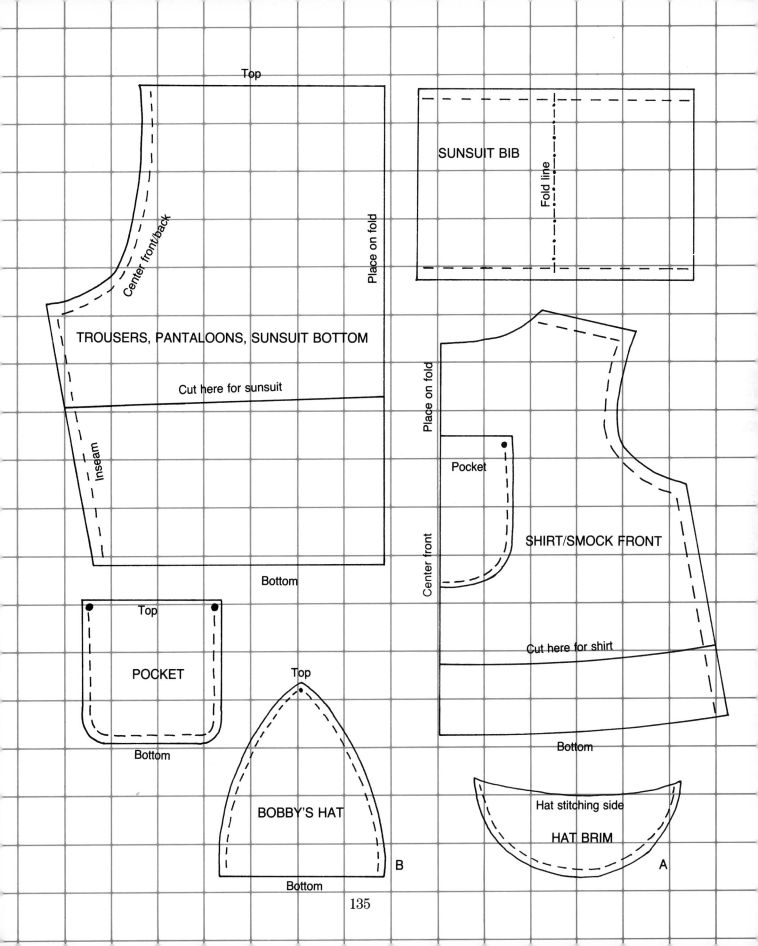

Top

Place on fold

Center front/back

TROUSERS, PANTALOONS, SUNSUIT BOTTOM

Cut here for sunsuit

Inseam

Bottom

SUNSUIT BIB

Fold line

Place on fold

Center front

Pocket

SHIRT/SMOCK FRONT

Cut here for shirt

Bottom

Top

POCKET

Bottom

Top

BOBBY'S HAT

Bottom

B

Hat stitching side

HAT BRIM

A

135

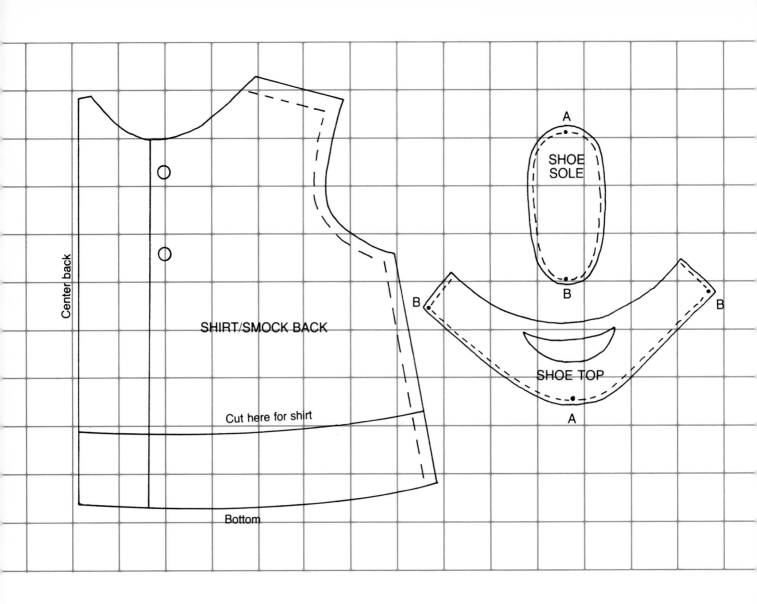

Center back

SHIRT/SMOCK BACK

Cut here for shirt

Bottom

A

SHOE SOLE

B

B

SHOE TOP

A

B

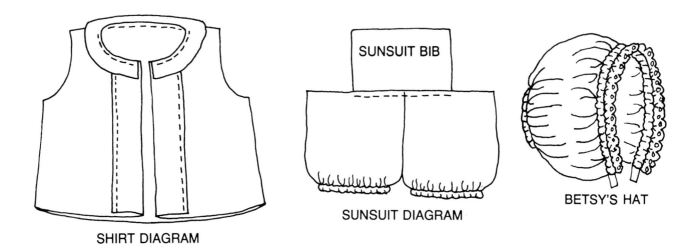

SHIRT DIAGRAM

SUNSUIT BIB

SUNSUIT DIAGRAM

BETSY'S HAT

Sailor Sam

Sailor Sam improves manual dexterity as your child dresses him in his sailor outfit and puts him into and takes him out of his boat. It is also a cheery toy that will stimulate your little one's imagination to pretend the living-room rug is an ocean to sail across.

MATERIALS FOR SAM AND WARDROBE

Cotton fabrics:
¼ yard 45"-wide pale peach
11" × 12" piece red gingham
11" × 12" piece red
11" × 14" piece white

5 ounces polyester stuffing
25 yards black yarn
2 yards #8 heavy-duty white thread
Two small snaps
1 yard each of six-strand red and black embroidery floss
Four ⅜" two-hole shirt buttons
12" piece ⅜"-wide satin ribbon
9½" piece ¼"-wide elastic
Thread to match fabrics

See How to Enlarge Patterns in General Directions, page 12.

Enlarge and cut pattern pieces from paper. Draw face on doll's head and mark all dots.

From peach fabric, cut two bodies, four arms, and four legs. Mark all dots.

Place body pattern under one body piece and trace face onto fabric. See Embroidery Stitches in General Directions, page 14. Backstitch mouth and nose with red floss and stitch freckles with French knots. With black floss, backstitch eyelashes. Fill in eyes with satin stitch.

All seams are ¼".

With right sides together stitch legs, leaving top edge open. Turn right side out and stuff.

Lining up the raw edges, baste legs to bottom edge of front doll piece. With right sides together stitch body pieces, leaving bottom edge open. Clip seam allowance at neck. Turn right side out and stuff. Slipstitch opening closed.

With right sides together stitch pairs of arms, leaving 2″ opening along one side for stuffing. Turn right side out and stuff. Slipstitch opening closed.

Lining up dots, place arm on each shoulder. Align buttons on top of arms and shoulder backs. With double strand #8 thread stitch through holes of buttons to secure arms to shoulders. See Diagram A.

Wrap yarn around 2″ × 20″ strip of paper. Machine-stitch lengthwise through center of strip. Clip yarn along folded edges and remove paper. Starting at center back of head, backstitch hair around head. See Sweet Dream Baby with Bunting, Diagram A, page 73.

To construct hat, cut two hat pieces from white fabric. With right sides together stitch, leaving bottom edge open. Turn right side out. Press bottom edge under 1½″. Zigzag-stitch along raw edge. Fold bottom edge up 1″ and press. See Diagram B. Tack hat to head along seamlines.

To construct trousers, cut two pants pieces from red fabric. With right sides together, stitch one side seam. Press seam open. Press, then stitch top edge under ½″ twice and bottom edges

under ¼″ twice.

Insert safety pin through end of elastic and push through waist casing. Secure each end to fabric with a few stitches. Stitch side seam and inside leg seam.

To construct shirt, cut two collar pieces from white fabric. From red gingham fabric cut two shirt fronts. Cut one shirt back. Mark dots.

With right sides together, stitch collar pieces along outside edge from dot to dot. Turn right side out and press. Topstitch ¼″ from outside edge.

With right sides together, stitch shirt fronts to shirt back along shoulder seams.

Stitch edges of center shirt front under ¼″. Press center fronts along fold line. See Diagram C. Lining up raw edges, stitch collar to right side of shirt.

Clip seam allowance and zigzag-stitch seam allowance to shirt neckline without catching collar in stitching. See Diagram D.

Press, then hem bottom shirt and sleeve edges under ¼″ twice. With right sides together, stitch shirt side seams. Turn right side out.

Following pattern, stitch two snaps to shirt front.

Tie ribbon into a bow. Stitch to center front below collar.

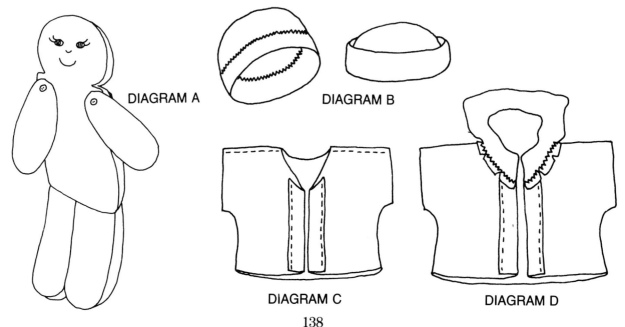

DIAGRAM A   DIAGRAM B

DIAGRAM C   DIAGRAM D

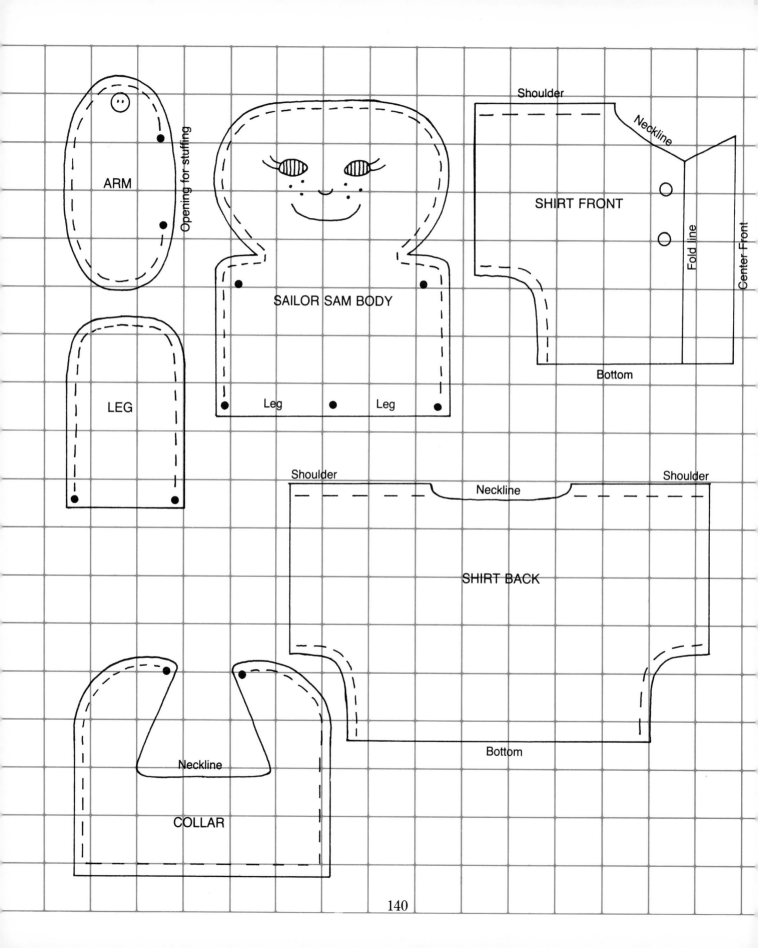

ARM

Opening for stuffing

SAILOR SAM BODY

Leg   Leg

LEG

SHIRT FRONT

Shoulder

Neckline

Fold line

Center Front

Bottom

Shoulder   Neckline   Shoulder

SHIRT BACK

Bottom

Neckline

COLLAR

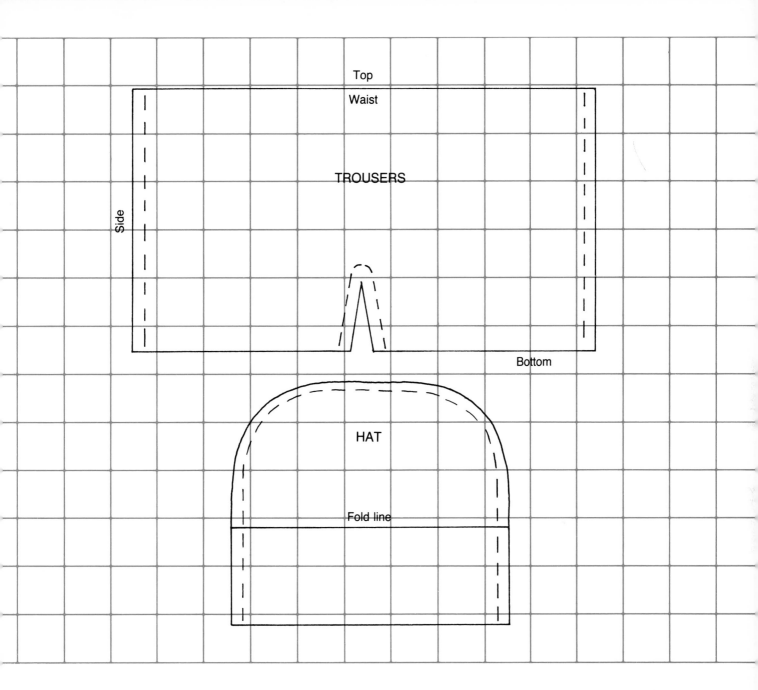

MATERIALS FOR BOAT

¼ yard 45″-wide blue cotton fabric
¼ yard 45″-wide interfacing
Extra-loft quilt batting:
4″ × 22″ piece
8″ × 12″ piece
Thread to match fabric

See How to Enlarge Patterns in General Directions, page 12.

Enlarge and cut boat bottom pattern from paper. From both blue fabric and interfacing folded double, cut boat bottom piece and one 6″ × 21″ rectangle. Unfold boat bottom pieces and adhere interfacing to fabric with hot iron.

Refold boat bottom and press. Press rectangle in half lengthwise.

Starting at top back, draw seven quilting lines 1″ apart on boat bottom. Draw two lengthwise quilting lines 1″ apart on rectangle. See Diagram E.

141

Sandwich 8″ × 12″ piece of batting between folded boat bottom piece, placing 8″ side of batting directly against fold. Baste layers together 1″ from outside edge. Starting at top back edge, topstitch over marked lines. Zigzag-stitch around outside raw edge of boat bottom. Trim excess batting.

Following pattern, mark fold line and topstitch over fold line marking.

Sandwich 4″ × 22″ piece of batting between fabric rectangle, placing 22″ side of batting directly against fold. Pin layers together; topstitch over marked lines. Zigzag-stitch around outside raw edge of rectangle. Trim excess batting. Mark vertical line through center of rectangle and topstitch.

With boat bottom folded up along fold line, stitch boat sides to boat bottom. See Diagram F.

See How to Bind Edges in General Directions, page 16.

On straight grain of blue fabric, cut two 2″ × 3½″ binding strips and one 2″ × 20″ strip.

Bind vertical back edges of boat with short strips and bottom edge with long strip.

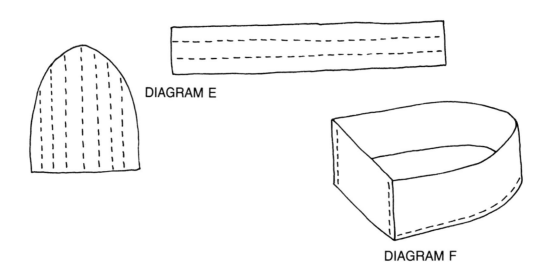

DIAGRAM E

DIAGRAM F

MATERIALS FOR FISH

9″ × 15″ piece green cotton fabric
2 yards six-strand black embroidery floss
Few handfuls polyester stuffing
Thread to match fabric

See How to Enlarge Patterns in General Directions, page 12.

Enlarge and cut pattern pieces from paper. Mark dots. Draw eye and mouth on fish pattern.

From fabric, cut two fish pieces, one gusset, and six fin pieces.

All seams are ⅛″.

With right sides together stitch pairs of fins, leaving body stitching side open. Turn right side out and press. Stuff each fin.

Lining up raw edges, baste one fin to top of right side of one fish piece between dots.

With right sides together, stitch top edge of fish pieces between A and B dots.

Lining up dots, stitch gusset to bottom of fish. Leave 2″ opening along one side for stuffing. Turn right side out and stuff. Slipstitch opening closed.

Turn raw edges of remaining fins under ¼″ and slipstitch to sides of fish.

See Embroidery Stitches in General Directions, page 14.

Following pattern, draw eyes and mouth on fish. Backstitch mouth and eyelashes with black floss. Fill in eyes with satin stitch.

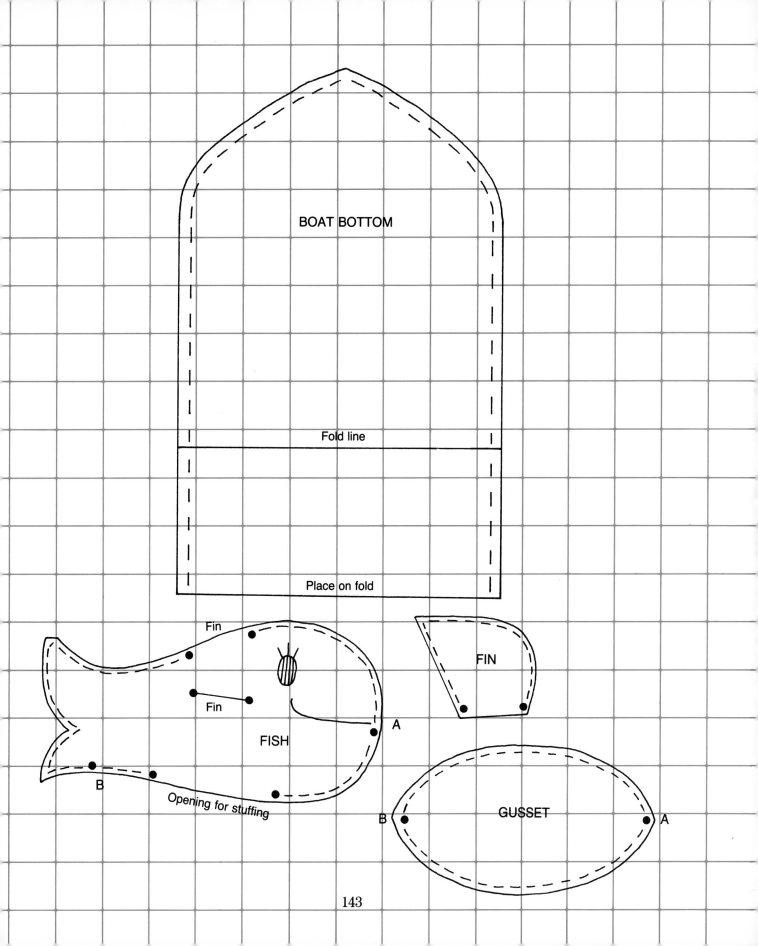

BOAT BOTTOM

Fold line

Place on fold

Fin

Fin

FISH

Opening for stuffing

A

B

FIN

GUSSET

B

A

143

Freddy the Frog

"Button my tie" is what Freddy would say if he could talk. Learning to button is a difficult task that takes lots of practice, but Freddy makes the learning fun. He appeals to a child's imagination while he teaches manual dexterity. And your youngster will find his silly-looking, lovable features irresistible.

MATERIALS

¼ yard green velour
¼ yard cotton print fabric
6″ × 6″ piece cotton print fabric
6″ × 6″ piece fusible interfacing
2″ × 4″ piece white felt
1½″ × 3″ piece black felt
1 yard ¼″-wide satin ribbon
10 ounces polyester stuffing
2 yards six-strand black embroidery floss
⅞″ shank button
Thread to match fabrics

See How to Enlarge Patterns in General Directions, page 12.

Enlarge and cut pattern pieces from paper. Draw eyes, nose, and mouth on head. Mark dots.

From velour folded double with nap running down, cut two head pieces and two pairs of arms and legs.

From ¼ yard cotton print folded double, mark, then cut four body pieces, two pairs boots, and one 3″ × 20″ strip for collar.

All seams are ¼″.

With right sides together, stitch boots to leg bottoms. Stitch pairs of legs, leaving top open for stuffing. Turn legs right side out and stuff.

With right sides together stitch arms, leaving top open for stuffing. Clip seam allowance around hands. Turn arms right side out and stuff.

With right sides together, stitch body center front and body center back seam. Lining up raw edges, baste arms and legs to body front between dots.

Stitch body front to back between A dots,

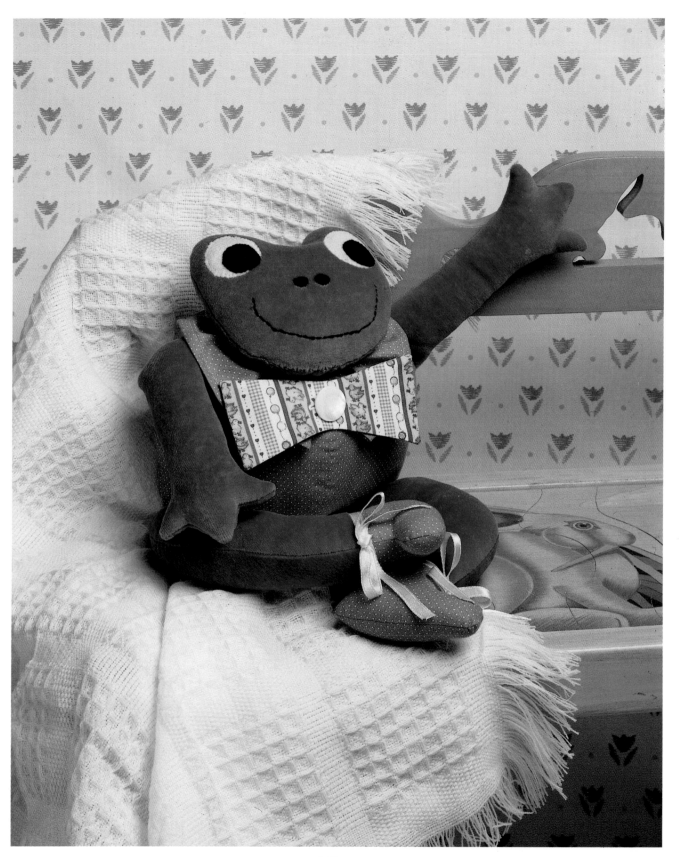

leaving bottom leg portion open. Turn right side out and stuff. Slipstitch opening closed.

With right sides together stitch head, leaving 2″ opening along bottom edge for stuffing. Clip seam allowance between eyes. Turn right side out and stuff.

Slipstitch head to shoulders of body front. See Diagram A.

Following pattern, cut two eyes from white felt and two pupils from black felt. Slipstitch into place on Freddy the Frog's face.

See Embroidery Stitches in General Directions, page 14.

Following pattern for placement, draw nostrils and mouth on Freddy the Frog's face. Fill in nostrils with satin stitch. Backstitch over mouth drawing.

To construct collar from 3″ × 20″ cotton strip, press two short sides and one long side under ¼″ twice. Hem. Gathering-stitch through remaining raw edge. Pull thread ends, gathering collar to fit snugly around Freddy the Frog's neck. Tie thread ends. With ends meeting at center front, slipstitch collar into place.

To construct bow tie, iron interfacing to 6″ × 6″ piece fabric. Fold fabric in half with right sides facing. Cut two bow tie pieces from fabric. Stitch raw edges, leaving 1″ opening for turning. Turn right side out and press. Slipstitch opening closed. Mark, then stitch 1″ buttonhole through center bow tie.

Securely stitch button to center front neck of Freddy the Frog. Button bow tie into place.

Divide ribbon into two equal pieces. Tie bow around each boot top. Secure bows by stitching a few stitches through center knot.

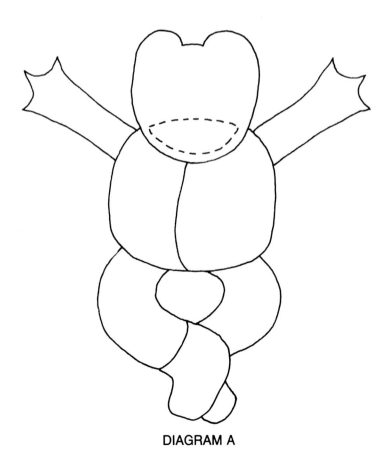

DIAGRAM A

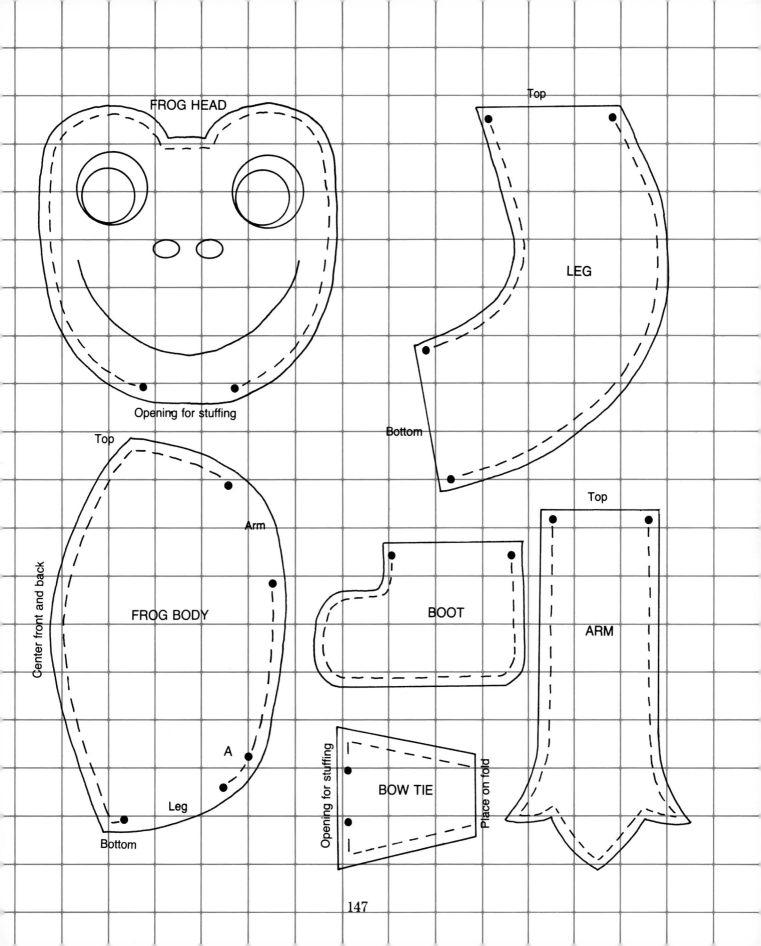

FROG HEAD

Opening for stuffing

Top

LEG

Bottom

Top

Top

Center front and back

Arm

FROG BODY

BOOT

ARM

A

Leg

Bottom

Opening for stuffing

BOW TIE

Place on fold

147

Getting Dressed Activity Block

This toy teaches your child to snap, zip, button, and fasten with Velcro. He will also learn to name and identify different articles of clothing. There are a lot of little but important things in one big block.

MATERIALS

¼ yard 45″-wide yellow cotton fabric

10 assorted cotton fabric scraps approximately 8″ × 8″

¼ yard 45″-wide fusible interfacing

⅜ yard ½″-wide lace

7″ zipper

2 medium-size snaps

½″ shank button

⅝″ round Velcro fastener

10 ounces polyester stuffing

Thread to match fabrics

See How to Enlarge Patterns in General Directions, page 12.

Enlarge and cut pattern pieces from paper.

From yellow fabric and interfacing, cut six 7″ × 7″ squares each. Fuse interfacing to fabric.

From fabric scraps, cut two pants pieces with two coordinating small pockets. Cut two shirt pieces with two coordinating small pockets. Cut two dress pieces with one coordinating small pocket. Cut one sunsuit piece and two straps. Cut one coordinating sunsuit top and small pocket. Cut one large pocket. Cut one 5″ × 5″ square and two 4″ × 4″ squares for hankies. Press, then zigzag-stitch hanky edges under ¼″.

All seams are ⅛″ unless otherwise specified.

Press all pocket edges under ¼″. Hem top edge of each pocket. Following pattern for placement, stitch small pockets to corresponding clothing pieces. Center and stitch large pocket to one yellow fabric panel.

To construct shirt panel, press all edges of right-side shirt piece under ¼″. Topstitch to a yellow panel. Press center front of left-side shirt

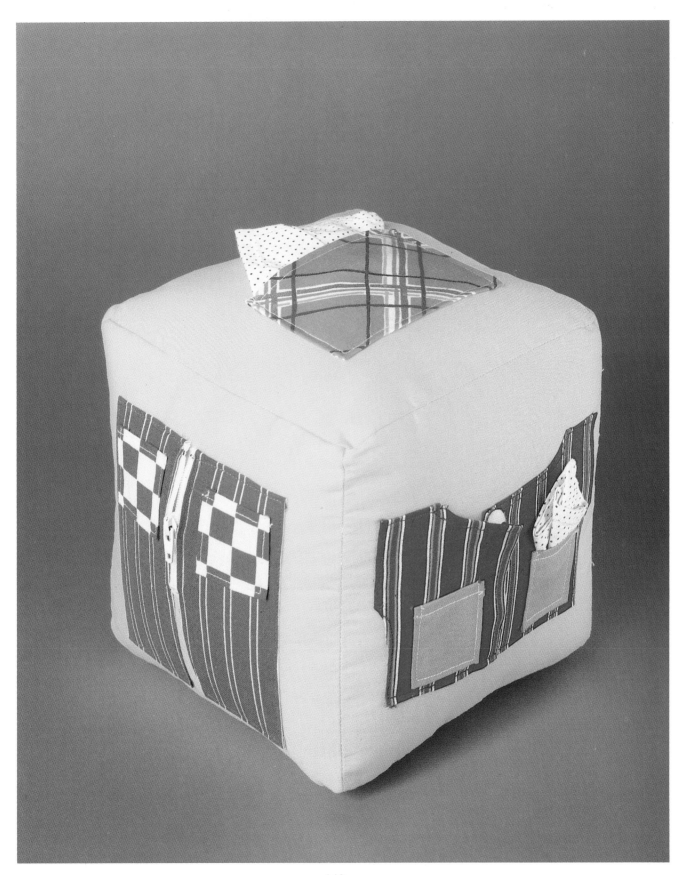

piece under ¾″ and remaining edges under ¼″. Hem center front with ⅝″ seam and neckline with ¼″ seam. With left-center front shirt overlapping right-center front shirt ½″, stitch left-side shirt to panel. Leave neckline and center front unstitched. Slipstitch Velcro fastener to center front opening. See Diagram A.

To construct dress panel, follow preceding instructions for shirt panel. Stitch ⅝″ button hole in left-side center-front dress piece before topstitching to panel. Topstitch dress pieces to panel leaving only top 2″ of center front unstitched. Stitch button to right-side dress piece. Stitch lace to sleeve edges and dress bottom. See Diagram B.

To construct pants panel, press center-front pants pieces on fold line and all remaining raw edges under ¼″.

To shorten zipper, close and trim zipper top directly above teeth. Stitch zipper teeth together securely 2½″ down from zipper top. Cut zipper ⅛″ below stitches.

Place zipper under folded center front of pants pieces and stitch into place. Center and stitch pants to a yellow panel. See Diagram C.

To construct sunsuit panel, press all edges of sunsuit top under ¼″. Stitch to a yellow panel. Press all edges of sunsuit under ¼″ and stitch to panel. Press one short side of straps under ¼″. Press long sides under ¼″. Fold straps in half lengthwise so folds meet. Topstitch straps along open folded edges. Stitch raw edge of straps to shoulders of sunsuit top. Stitch snaps to strap bottoms and bib of sunsuit. See Diagram D.

To construct block, with right sides facing, stitch four panels together along their vertical sides, with ¼″ seam. Reserve large pocket panel for top and empty panel for bottom. Press seams open.

With right sides together, stitch top panel to block sides. See Diagram E. Stitch bottom panel, leaving 5″ opening along one side for turning. Turn right side out and stuff. Slipstitch opening closed.

Insert large hanky into large pocket and small hankies into small pockets.

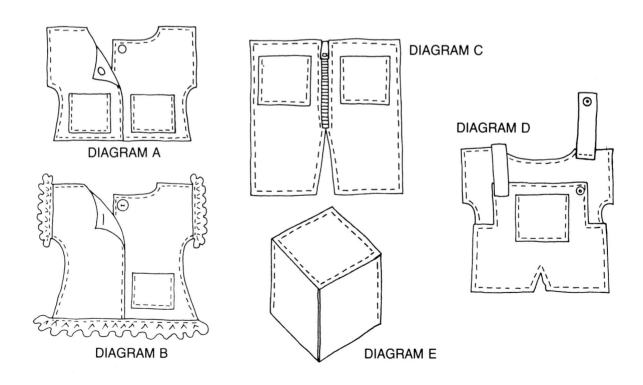

DIAGRAM A

DIAGRAM B

DIAGRAM C

DIAGRAM D

DIAGRAM E

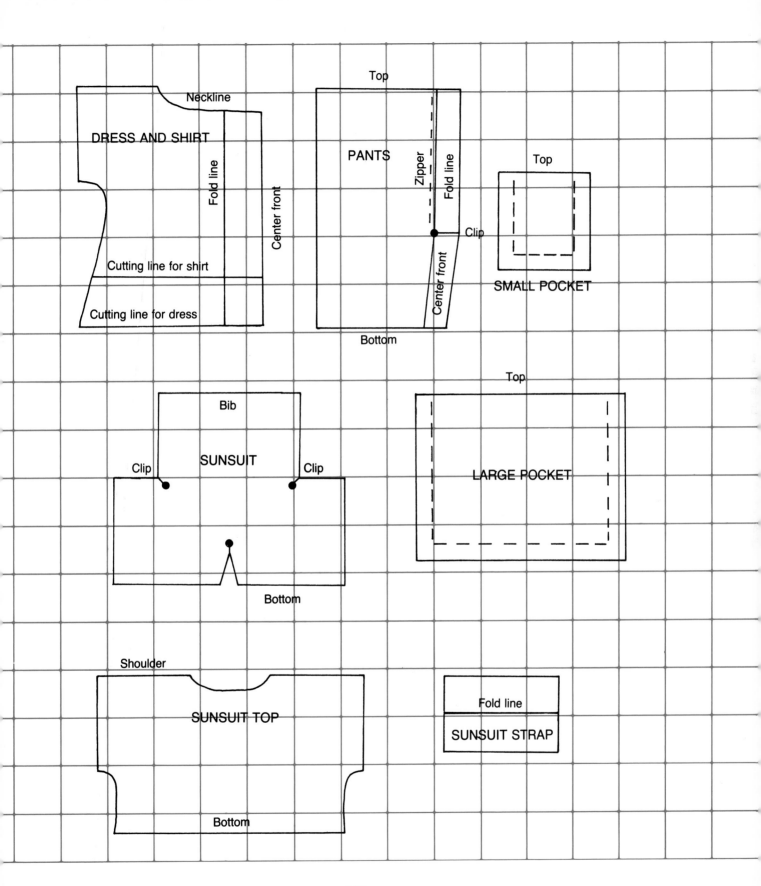

Topsy-Turvy Sue

This two-sided doll is based on a classic American folk-art design that has been popular for many decades. You can use Sue to teach your child to recognize happy and sad feelings. It is also fun for peekaboo play. It's a simple toy that never seems to lose its appeal.

MATERIALS

9″ × 22″ piece off-white robe velour
¼ yard 45″-wide cotton print
¼ yard 45″-wide cotton print (coordinating color)
4 yards yellow yarn
1 yard 1″-wide lace
½ yard ⅜″-wide satin ribbon
Six-strand blue and pink embroidery floss
6 ounces polyester stuffing
Thread to match fabrics

Trace and cut pattern pieces from paper. Draw features on face and mark dots.

With velour folded double, cut two pairs of heads and four pairs of arms. From either ¼ yard cotton print cut two body pieces, leaving 9″ × 36″ rectangle of fabric.

Cut 9″ × 36″ rectangle from remaining ¼ yard of print fabric.

Following pattern diagram, draw happy face on one head piece with chalk. Draw sad face on another head by inverting mouth.

See Embroidery Stitches in General Directions, page 14.

Backstitch over mouth and nose drawings with pink floss. Fill in eyes with blue satin stitch.

Divide yarn into two equal pieces. Wrap each

piece around 1″ × 3″ strip of paper. Stitch length-wise across paper ¼″ from edge. Remove paper. Fold yarn strip in half. Lining up raw edge of fabric with stitched side of yarn, baste yarn between dots to right-side seam allowance of each embroidered head. See Diagram A.

All seams are ¼″ unless otherwise specified.

With right sides together, stitch embroidered head pieces to top and bottom of one body piece between dots. Stitch remaining head pieces to top and bottom of other body piece.

With right sides together stitch doll, leaving 3″ opening along one side for stuffing. Clip neck seam allowance. Turn doll right side out and stuff. Slipstitch opening closed.

With right sides together, stitch pairs of arms with ⅛″ seam allowance, leaving 1″ opening along one side for stuffing. Clip seam allowance between thumb and forefinger. Turn right side out and stuff. Slipstitch opening closed. Using double thread, tack an arm securely to each shoulder,

stitching completely through arm and shoulder with ¼″ stitches.

To construct skirt, press one 36″ side of each fabric rectangle under ¼″.

With right sides together, stitch unfolded 36″ sides with ⅛″ seam allowance.

Press seam allowance to one side and run a gathering stitch along opposite side ⅛″ from seam.

Stitch side seam. Press seam open. See Diagram B.

Place doll body inside skirt tube, positioning gathering stitch at waistline. Pull thread ends, gathering skirt until it fits snugly around waist. Stitching over gathering stitches, backstitch skirt into place.

Bring folded bottom edges of skirt together, sandwiching lace between fabric. Topstitch layers together ⅛″ from folded edges of fabric.

Divide ribbon into two equal pieces. Tie each into a bow. Stitch bow to top of each head.

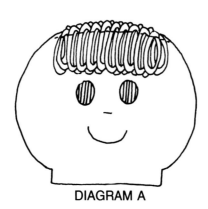

DIAGRAM A

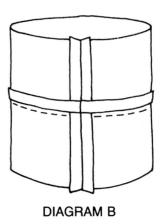

DIAGRAM B

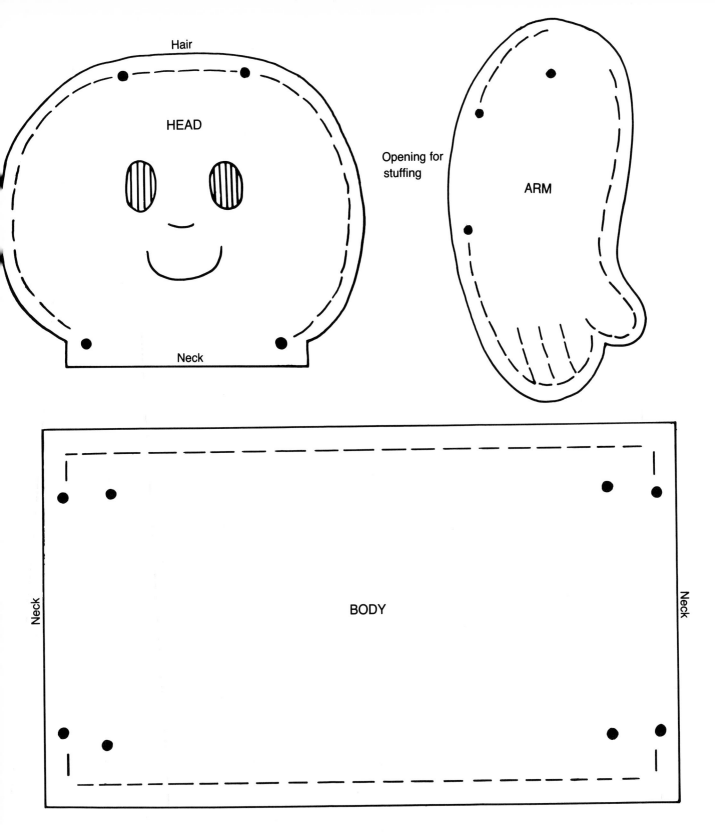

Hair

HEAD

Neck

Opening for
stuffing

ARM

Neck

BODY

Neck

FULL SIZE—DO NOT ENLARGE

Little Red Mouse House

This house is full of fun for tots of all sizes. It belongs to a family of mommy and daddy and baby mice. Your child can look and find them inside the house or take them out to play.
The toy teaches the concept of large and small. It also teaches object permanence—when the mice are hidden inside the house, they haven't ceased to exist.
Children find mice very appealing, perhaps because they're little too and have high, squeaky voices. These will be a special variety because you made them.

MATERIALS

Cotton fabrics:
8½" × 14½" piece red
6" × 6" piece yellow
9" × 20" piece orange with white dots

9" × 30" piece green quilted fabric
12" strip fusible tape
4 handfuls polyester stuffing
1 yard black yarn
1½ yards six-strand black embroidery floss
¾" × 1" Velcro strip
Red and yellow sewing thread

See How to Enlarge Patterns in General Directions, page 12.

Enlarge and cut pattern pieces from paper. Draw eyes and nose on mice.

From red fabric rectangle, measure and use chalk to mark a parallel line 6" away from 8½" side to make house-front fold line.

Cut two windows and one door from yellow fabric. Using small pieces of fusible web, center and adhere door to rectangle. Place bottom of door on chalk line. Adhere windows to rectangle ¼" away from door sides and 1" up from chalk line. See Diagram A. Using closely spaced zigzag

stitch, machine-appliqué door and windows onto rectangle.

From quilted fabric, cut one roof piece.

All seams are ¼″.

With right sides together, stitch top roof edge to bottom of house rectangle. See Diagram B.

From quilted fabric, cut 9″ × 20″ rectangle. Place stitched house piece right sides together with rectangle. Stitch around outside edge of house piece, leaving 4½″ opening along one side for turning and being careful not to catch roof edge in stitching. Trim excess quilted fabric. Turn house right side out. Slipstitch opening closed.

Machine-topstitch along house-front fold line and ⅛″ from roof seam.

With wrong sides together and folding house on fold line, slipstitch sides together. See Diagram C.

Center and stitch Velcro to inside roof opening.

To construct each large mouse, cut two body and four paw pieces from orange fabric.

See Embroidery Stitches in General Directions, page 14.

Following pattern for placement, and using black floss, mark, then stitch eyes and nose with French knots.

To stitch whiskers, tie knot in floss end and push needle through wrong side of fabric. Clip thread to 1″ in length. Stitch three whiskers on each cheek.

For tail, cut 8″ piece yarn. Tie knot in each end. Stitch one end to center of right-side seam allowance of back mouse piece.

With right sides together stitch mouse body, leaving 1½″ opening along bottom edge.

Clip seam allowance around ears. Turn right side out and stuff. Slipstitch opening closed.

With right sides together stitch paws, leaving straight side open. Turn right side out; stuff lightly. Turn raw edges under ⅛″. Slipstitch opening closed. Following pattern for placement, slipstitch paws to mouse body.

To construct baby mouse follow preceding instructions, making tail 5″ and omitting paws.

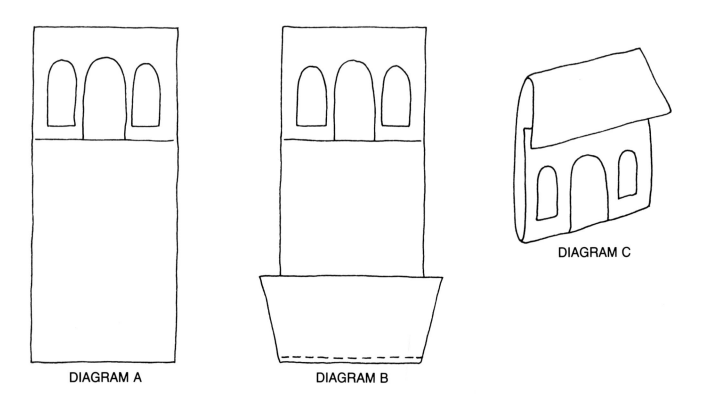

DIAGRAM A

DIAGRAM B

DIAGRAM C

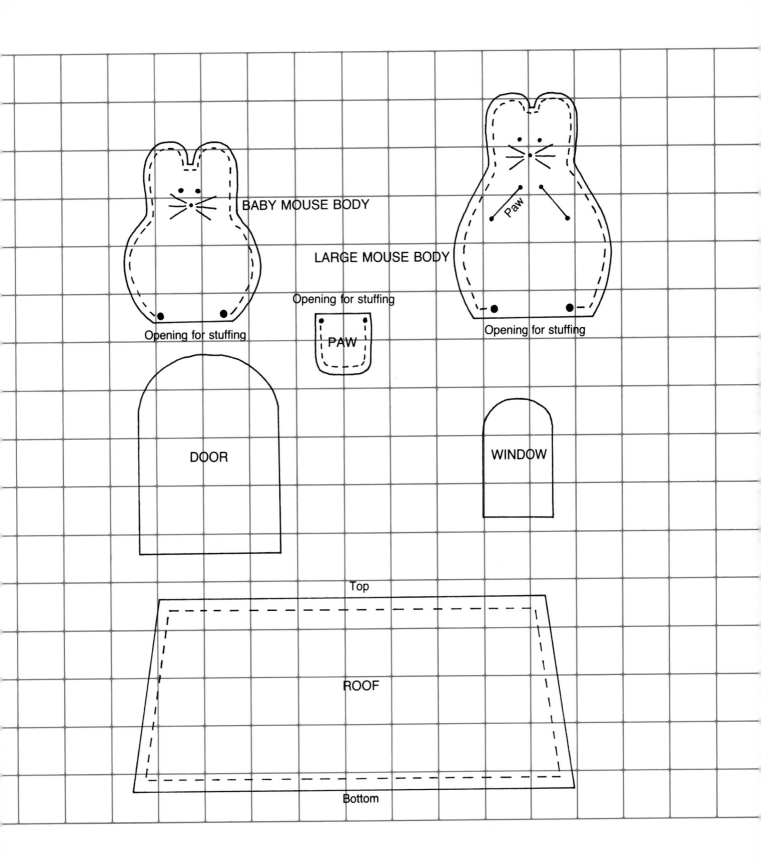

BABY MOUSE BODY

LARGE MOUSE BODY

Paw

Opening for stuffing

Opening for stuffing

PAW

Opening for stuffing

Opening for stuffing

DOOR

WINDOW

Top

ROOF

Bottom

159

Polly Penguin and Chick

Here is a toy that will remain your child's companion as he grows. Baby chick unfastens from Polly Penguin. By placing the chick in mother's wings and then taking it out, your baby will improve his manual dexterity and coordination.

For a toddler, this toy introduces the concept of size: large and small. And the child learns that baby is truly a separate person from mommy. Polly Penguin and Chick encourage baby to begin independent exploration of the environment.

MATERIALS

⅓ yard 60″-wide black velour
9″ × 11″ piece white velour
9″ × 12″ piece orange cotton fabric
¾″ × 1″ piece black Velcro strip
3″ × 5″ piece fusible interfacing
12 ounces polyester stuffing
Thread to match fabrics

See How to Enlarge Patterns in General Directions, page 12.

Enlarge and cut pattern pieces from paper. Mark all dots and feather stitching lines on wings (broken lines). Draw eyes on front head patterns.

To construct Polly Penguin, cut two back pieces and one head front piece from black velour with nap running down. Cut one bottom piece. With velour folded double, cut two pairs of wings. Mark all dots.

From white velour with nap running down, cut one body front piece. Mark dots. From orange cotton, cut two beak and four foot pieces. All seams are ¼″.

With right sides together stitch beak and feet, leaving straight sides open. Clip foot seam allowances. Turn pieces right side out and stuff.

Lining up raw edges, baste beak to front head between dots. With right sides together, machine-stitch front head to front body. With right sides together, stitch back pieces along center back edge between dots A and B, leaving 4″ opening for stuffing.

Lining up dots A, stitch penguin front to penguin back pieces, stitching from A to penguin bottom. See Diagram A.

Lining up raw edges, baste feet to front body between dots.

With right sides together, line up dot C on bottom piece with center back seam and stitch bottom piece to penguin body.

With right sides together stitch wings, leaving 3″ opening along one side for stuffing. Turn right side out and stuff lightly. Slipstitch opening closed. Following broken lines on pattern, topstitch feathers on wings.

Following Diagram B, slipstitch wings to penguin. Stitch along back edge of wing. Wing tips should overlap by approximately 3″. Hand stitch Velcro to tip of wings.

To construct eyes, divide fusible interfacing into 3″ × 3″ and 2″ × 3″ pieces. Fuse 3″ × 3″ piece to white velour and 2″ × 3″ piece to black velour. Using drawing from front head pattern, cut out two white eyes and two black pupils. Slipstitch securely into place on Polly Penguin's head.

To construct chick, cut one chick back and head front piece from black velour with nap running down. Fold fabric double and cut two pairs of wings. From white velour, cut one body front piece. From orange cotton, cut two beak and four foot pieces.

All seams are ⅛″.

With right sides together stitch beak and pairs of feet, leaving straight sides open. Turn right side out and stuff.

Lining up raw edges, baste beak to head front between dots and feet to body front between dots.

With right sides together, stitch head front to body front. Stitch penguin front to penguin back, leaving bottom edge open. Turn right side out and stuff. Slipstitch opening closed.

With right sides together stitch wings, leaving 1″ opening along one side for turning. Turn right side out. Slipstitch opening closed. Following broken lines on pattern, topstitch feathers on wings. Stitching along top and halfway down back edge of wings, slipstitch wings to chick.

Using drawing from front head pattern, cut two white eyes and two black pupils from fused velour. Slipstitch eyes securely into place on chick.

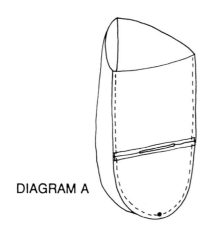

DIAGRAM A

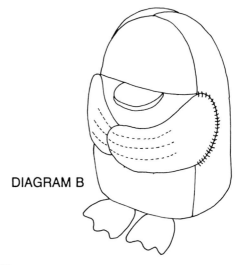

DIAGRAM B

162

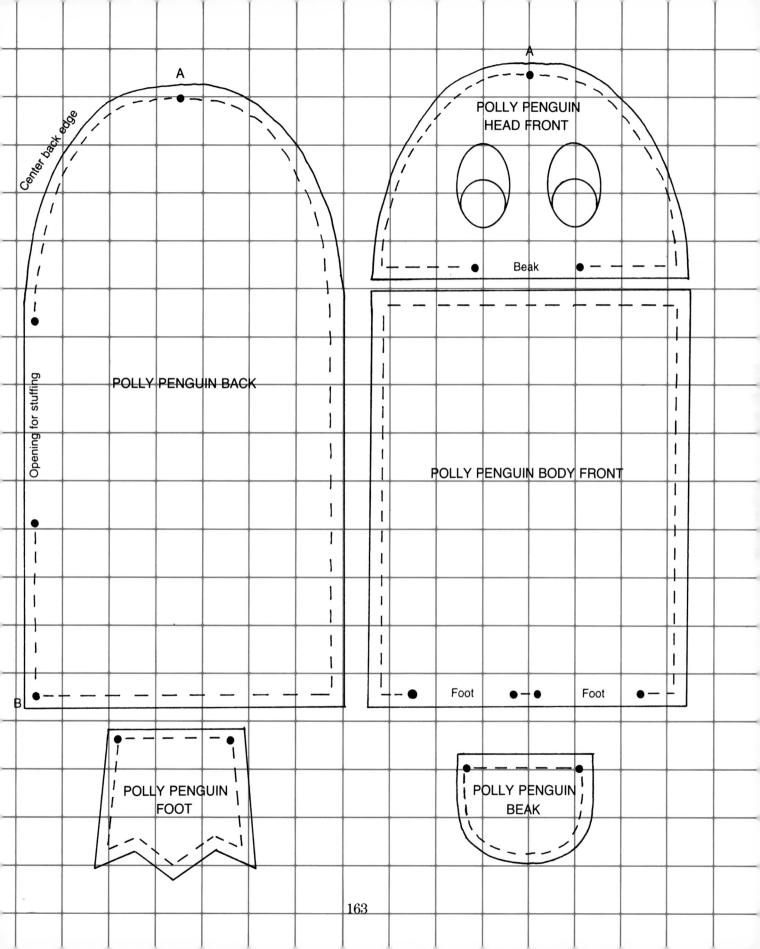

A

POLLY PENGUIN
HEAD FRONT

Beak

Center back edge

Opening for stuffing

POLLY PENGUIN BACK

POLLY PENGUIN BODY FRONT

B

Foot   Foot

POLLY PENGUIN
FOOT

POLLY PENGUIN
BEAK

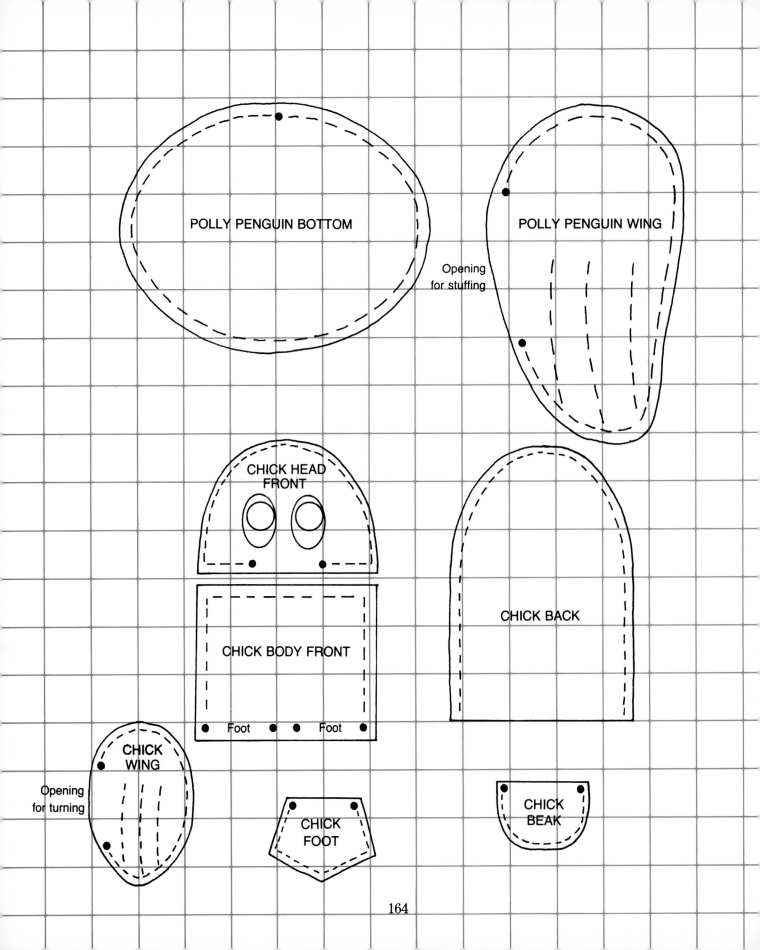

POLLY PENGUIN BOTTOM

POLLY PENGUIN WING

Opening
for stuffing

CHICK HEAD
FRONT

CHICK BACK

CHICK BODY FRONT

Foot   Foot

CHICK
WING

Opening
for turning

CHICK
FOOT

CHICK
BEAK

164

Index

Index to Toys

with Age Recommendations

Because all children are unique, this listing is only a general guide. While infants may enjoy a toy at one level, older children will use it in another way. In playing with your child, you will discover which activity is best suited for your own baby or child.